John Gough Nichols, Edward Francis Rimbault

Two sermons preached by the boy bishop at St. Paul's

John Gough Nichols, Edward Francis Rimbault

Two sermons preached by the boy bishop at St. Paul's

ISBN/EAN: 9783744744928

Printed in Europe, USA, Canada, Australia, Japan

Cover: Foto ©Lupo / pixelio.de

More available books at **www.hansebooks.com**

TWO SERMONS

PREACHED BY

THE BOY BISHOP

AT

ST. PAUL'S, TEMP. HENRY VIII., AND AT GLOUCESTER, TEMP. MARY.

EDITED BY JOHN GOUGH NICHOLS, F.S.A.

WITH AN INTRODUCTION GIVING AN ACCOUNT

OF

THE FESTIVAL OF THE BOY BISHOP

IN ENGLAND,

BY EDWARD F. RIMBAULT, LL.D.,

&c., &c.

PRINTED FOR THE CAMDEN SOCIETY.

M.DCCC.LXXV.

TO THE READER.

THE subject of the following pages, it is well known, for many years engaged the attention of the late Mr. John Gough Nichols, who desired to give an exhaustive account of one of the most ancient and interesting festivals of our forefathers—interesting on many accounts, but particularly so from its bearing upon the education of our early choristers. Unfortunately Mr. Nichols did not live to carry out his intentions. Had he done so, the members of the Camden Society would have been in possession of a far different work from that now presented to them.

Mr. Nichols had made considerable collections for a history of the festival of the Boy Bishop throughout Europe, but, upon these papers being handed over to me, it was found that they were jottings, to be investigated at leisure, and would take months, nay perhaps years, to work out with any degree of satisfaction. Under these circumstances all that could be done was to confine my remarks to the Boy Bishop in England—a subject to which I had given some little attention—and to prefix them to the two Sermons which Mr. Nichols had already prepared for the press. In so doing I have availed myself of several of that gentleman's remarks,

which are duly acknowledged in their proper places. I have also
prefixed a short bibliographical and biographical preface to the
Sermons, and have added a curious document (found among Mr.
Nichols's papers) as an Appendix. For the few notes to the latter,
the members are indebted to the late Dr. Rock, the learned author
of "The Church of our Fathers." And I may refer the reader to
Brand's Popular Antiquities [a] for some general information on the
subject.

To my kind friend William Chappell, Esq., F.S.A., I must
express my obligations for his translation of part of the York
Computus (pp. 11-15), which Mr. Nichols had left unfinished, and
for many valuable suggestions throughout the work.

EDWARD F. RIMBAULT.

29, St. Mark's Crescent, Regent's Park, N.W.
Midsummer 1875.

[a] Vol. 1, ed. 1849, p. 421.

INTRODUCTION.

In the middle ages festivities were a part of human existence into which all classes entered with hearty interest. The song and the dance, and the rude drama, were not confined within the walls of the hall or theatre, but they were familiar to the public ear and the public gaze in the open market-place and at the corners of the streets. They were attendant on the processions of the Church and the pageantry of the guilds, and regularly succeeded the more important business of life as one day followed another. Throughout the year, except during Lent, there was a constant series of holidays, kept in commemoration of the saints; and those days, by religion and by custom, were divided between sacred rites and secular discussions, each portion of such celebration combining a large amount of ceremonial, pomp, and parade.

The saints were all invested with special attributes and special claims to worship and adoration. They were intercessors not only in mental distresses and anxieties, in physical pains and diseases, and in accidental misfortunes and losses,—not to speak of the aspirations of ambition or worldliness, upon which Erasmus has inflicted such amusing satire,—but to each of them, according to their respective character and merits, was attributed a tutelary influence over localities, seasons, and circumstances; over every variety of worldly occupation, and over even sports and pastimes.

The Festival of St. Nicholas, observed on the 6th of December, was marked by several pecularities which connect the saint with the marine deities of Scandinavia, of Greece, and of Rome. He is said by Moreri to have been Bishop of Myra in the fourth century, and he was accounted a saint of the highest virtue, even in his earliest infancy. This saint has ever been considered the patron of scholars and of youth, for which a reason has been assigned by the Rev. W. Cole, from a Life of Saint Nicholas printed in 1645 (3rd edit.): "An Asiatic gentleman, sending his two sons to Athens for education, ordered them to wait on the Bishop for his benediction. On arriving at Myra with their baggage they took up their lodgings at an inn, proposing to defer their visit till the morrow; but in the mean time the innkeeper, to secure their effects to himself, killed the young gentlemen, cut them into pieces, salted them, and intended to sell them for pickled pork. St. Nicholas being favoured with a sight of these proceedings in a vision, went to the inn, and reproached the landlord with the crime, who, immediately confessing it, entreated the saint to pray to Heaven for his pardon. The Bishop, moved by his confession and contrition, besought forgiveness for him and supplicated restoration of life to the children. Scarcely had he finished when the pieces reunited, and the resuscitated youths threw themselves from the brine tub at the feet of the Bishop: he raised them up, blessed them, and sent them to Athens, with great joy, to prosecute their studies."[a]

The most important feature of the festival of St. Nicholas was the election of the BOY-BISHOP, *Episcopus Puerorum, Episcopus Choristarum.* This festival was not confined to one country, and, of course, therefore, it may be easily imagined that it assumed a very different complexion according to time and place, being in one locality of a serious character, and in another verging closely on the burlesque. The best account we

---

[a] Hone, Ancient Mysteries, p. 193. See a good account of the legends connected with St. Nicholas in Hampson's Medii Ævi Kalendarium, i. 66 *et seq.*

have of it in the first of these forms is from the learned John Gregory, whose attention was called to the subject by happening to find that " in the cathedral of Sarum there lieth a monument in stone, of a little boie habited all in episcopal robes, a miter upon his head, a crosier in his hand, and the rest accordingly. The monument lay long buried under the seats near the pulpit, at the removal whereof it was of late years discovered, and translated from thence to the north part of the nave, where it now lieth betwixt the pillars, covered over with a box of wood, not without a general imputation of raritie and reverence, it seeming almost impossible to everie one, that either a bishop could bee so small in person, or a childe so great in clothes." Finding that he could obtain no solution of this mystery from the learned, Gregory obtained a sight of the old statutes of the Cathedral, and was fortunate enough to find one amongst them with the title DE EPISCOPO CHORISTARUM —*of the Chorister-Bishop.* This referred him to the *Sarum Proces-sionale,* in which he found the following minute and curious description of the ceremony: " The Episcopus Choristarum was a chorister-bishop chosen by his fellow children upon St. Nicholas' daie . . . . From this daie till Innocents' day at night (it lasted longer at the first), the *Episcopus Puerorum* [Boy-Bishop] was to bear the name and hold up the state of a bishop, answerably habited, with a crosier or pastoral staff in his hand, and a miter upon his head; and such an one too som had, as was *multis episcoporum mitris sumtuosior,* saith one—verie much richer than those of bishops indeed. The rest of his fellows from the same time beeing were to take upon them the style and counterfaict of prebends, yielding to their bishops (or els as if it were) no less then canonical obedience. And look what service the verie bishop himself with his dean and prebends (had they been to officiate) was to have performed, the mass excepted, the verie same was don by the chorister-bishop and his canons upon this Eve and the Holiedaie. By the use of Sarum,—for 'tis almost the onely place where I can hear anie thing of this,[a]—that of York in their *Processional* seemeth to take no notice of it—upon the Eve to Innocents' daie the chorister-bishop was to go in solemn procession with his fellows *ad altare Sanctæ Trinitatis et omnium Sanctorum* (as the PROCESSIONAL—or *ad altare Innocentium sive Sanctæ Trinitas*, as the PIE[b]) *in capis, et cereis ardentibus in manibus*, in their copes, and burning tapers in their hands, the bishop beginning and the other boies following, *Centum quadraginta quatuor*, &c. Then the vers, *Hi empti sunt ex omnibus*, &c. And this is sang by three of the boies. Then all the boies sing the PROSA[c] *Sedentem in supernæ majestatis arce*, &c. The chorister-bishop in the meantime fumeth the altar first, and then the image of the Holie Trinitie. Then the bishop saith, *modesta voce*, the verse *Lætamini;* and the respond is *Et gloriamini*, &c. Then the praier which wee yet retain—*Deus cujus hodierna die*, &c. But the rubrick to the pie saith, *sacerdos dicat*, both the praier and the lætamini—that is, som rubricks do; otherwise I take the benediction to bee of more priestlie consequence then the *oremus*, &c., which yet was solemnly performed by the chorister-bishop, as will follow. In their return from the altar, *præcentor puerorum incipiat*, &c.—the chanter-chorister is to begin—De Sancta Maria, &c. The respond is *Felix namque*, &c. Sic processio, &c. The procession was made into the quire by the west door, and in such order (as it should seem by Molanus) that

[a] This is a somewhat extraordinary statement to make, for Gregory had the reputation of being a man of research. The custom of electing a Boy Bishop was universal.

[b] The PIE was the old Romish Ordinal, in Latin called Pica. "Ordinale quod usitato dicitur Pica sive Directorium Sacerdotum."

[c] The PROSA or PROSE is a name for certain songs of rejoicing, chanted before the gospel, and so called because the regular laws of metre are not observed in them.

the dean and canons went foremost, the chaplains next, the bishop
with his little prebends in the last and highest place. The bishop
taketh his seat, and the rest of the children dispose of themselves
upon each side of the quire upon the uppermost ascent, the canons
resident bearing the incens and the book, and the petit canons the
tapers, according to the rubrick. And from this hour to the full
end of the next daies procession, none of the clergy, whatever may
be their rank, ascend to the upper seats.

" Then the bishop from his seat says the vers, *Speciosus formâ,*
&c. *Diffusa est gratia labiis tuis.* Then the praier, *Deus qui
salutis æternæ,* &c. *Pax vobis.* Then, after the *Benedicamus Domino,*
the bishop of the children sitting in his seat is to give the benediction, or bless the people in this manner : *Princeps Ecclesiæ, pastor
ovilis, cunctam plebem tuam benedicere digneris,* &c. Then turning
towards the people hee singeth or saith (for all this was in plano
cantu ; that age was so far from skilling discants or the fuges
that they were not come up to counterpoint) *Cum mansuetudine
humilitate vos ad benedictionem,* the chorus answering *Deo gratias.*
Then the cross-bearer delivereth up the crosier to the bishop again,
and then the bishop, having first crossed his forehead, says, *Adjutorium nostrum in nomine Domini,* the chorus answering *qui
fecit cælum et terram.* Then, after some other like ceremonies
performed, the Episcopus Puerorum, or chorister-bishop, begineth
the *Completorium* or *Complyn,* and that don he turneth towards
the quire and saith, *Adjutorium,* &c. Then last of all he saith,
Benedicat vos omnipotens Deus pater, et filius, et spiritus sanctus.

" ON INNOCENTS' DAY, *at the second vespers, let the cross-bearer
receive the crosier of the boy-bishop, and let them sing the antiphon
as at the first vespers. Likewise let the boy-bishop bless the people
in the way above-mentioned, and the service of this day be thus
fulfilled.* (RUBRIC PROCESSIONAL). And all this was don with

CAMD. SOC. *b*

that solemnitie of celebration and appetite of seeing that the statute
of Sarum was forced to provide that no man whatsoever, under the
pain of anathema, should interrupt or press upon these children at
the procession spoken of before, or in anie other part of their
service in anie waies, but to suffer them quietly to perform and
execute what it concerned them to do. And the part was acted
yet more earnestly, for Molanus saith that this bishop in some
places did receive rents, capons, &c. during his year, &c.; and it
seemeth by the statute of Sarum that hee held a kind of visitation,
and had a full corespondencie of all other state and prerogative.
More then all this, Molanus[a] tells us of a chorister-bishop in the
church of Cambraie who disposeth of a prebend which fell void
in his moneth (or year, for I know not which it was) to his master.
In case the chorister-bishop died within the moneth, his exsequies
were solemnized with an answerable glorious pomp and sadness.
He was buried, as all other bishops, in all his ornaments, as by
the monument of stone, spoken of before, it plainly appeareth."[b]

. After having performed the functions of a bishop within his own
cathedral church and city, the next part the boy-bishop had to play
was that of making a visitation. That this was not unusual we
learn from the Northumberland Household Book, in which it is
mentioned that the Earl was annually accustomed to entertain the
boy-bishop of York and Beverley, and from the notice we have of
the boy-bishop at Winchester.[c] The privilege was in some instances

---

[a] "D. Joannes de Molanus, De Historia S. Imaginum de Picturarum," 12mo.
Lugduni, 1619.

[b] "Episcopus Puerorum, in Die Innocentium; or, A Discourse of an Antient
Custom in the Church of Sarum, making an anniversarie Bishop among the
Choristers." Pages 95-123 in Gregorii Posthuma; or Certain Learned Tracts
written by John Gregorie, 4to. Lond. 1649.

[c] "It was upon this festival that some wealthy man or another of the parish
would make an entertainment on the occasion for his own household, and invite his
neighbours' children to come and partake of it; and of course Nicholas and his

restrained; as when Bishop Mortival, at Salisbury, in 1319, forbad
for the future both feast and visitation (*convivium aliquod de cetero
vel visitationem exterius vel interius nullatenus faciendo*); and as when
Bishop Grandison in the statutes for his college at Ottery St. Mary
declared that the boys were not to be allowed on the feast of the
Holy Innocents to wander beyond the parish of Ottery. But a
York Computus, A.D. 1396, gives a very circumstantial account of
the visitation made by the boy-bishop in that year. This curious
roll, in the possession of Canon Raine, was lent to the late Mr.
J. G. Nichols, and from it he constructed a short narrative of the
boy-bishop's progress, which will be read with interest from the
minuteness of its details, and the graphic character of some of its
descriptions. As Canon Raine justly observes, " It is unique, and
throws more light upon the subject than anything that has yet
been seen."

The roll purports to be " The Account of Nicholas of Newark,
guardian of the property of John de Cave, boy-bishop in the year of
our Lord [13]96." The Receipts were derived partly from offerings
in the cathedral church, partly from the contributions of the canons,
and partly from the gifts of the nobility and of the monasteries which
the bishop visited. They are in the accompt divided under three
heads: the first containing the following: From the offerings on
Christmas day, xij d.; offerings on Innocents' day, xxiv s. j d., with
a silver spoon weighing xx d., a silver ring and a silk purse; from
William de Kexby the precentor, xx d.; from master John de Schir-

clerks sat in the highest place. The *Golden Legend* tells how 'a man, for the love
of his sone that went to scole for to lerne, halowed every year the feast of Saynt
Nycholas moche solemply. On a tyme it happed that the fader had to make redy
the dyner, and called many clerkes to this diner.' (Wynkyn de Worde, Lond. 1527.)
Individuals sometimes bequeathed money to find a yearly dinner on St. Nicholas's
day for as many as a hundred scholars, who were, after that, to pray for the soul of
the founder of the feast."—Dr. Rock's *Church of our Fathers*, iii. part 2, 216.

burne, the chancellor, ij s.; from master John de Newton, treasurer
ad Novam,* vj s. viij d.; from master Thomas Dalby, Archdeacon of
Richmond, vj s. viij d.; from master Nicholas de Feriby, vj s. viij d.;
and from master Thomas de Wallworth, vj s. viij d.; total, lv s. v d.
Secondly, in the town were received: from the Lord Abbot of
St. Mary's without the Walls of York, vj s. viij d.; and from master
William de Feriby, Archdeacon of the East Riding, iij s. iv d.;
total, x s. But the largest receipts arose from "the country:" being
the gifts of those to whom the bishop went in his visitation. They
amounted in all to v l. x s.: the particular donations we shall see in
following the bishop's progress. Altogether the receipts amounted
to viij l. xv s. v d.

The expenses commenced on the 23rd of December, when *O
Virgo virginum* was sung, and then j d. was spent in bread for wafer,
and vj d. in ale.

Within the city various purchases were made for the use of the
bishop: a torch weighing twelve pounds cost iv s. iij d.; a cap,
ix d.; a pair of linen gloves, iij d.; a pair of sleeves or cuffs, iij d.;
a pair of knives, xiv d.; a pair of spurs, v d.; for the making of his
gown, xviij d.; lamb's wool bought for his overcoat, ij s. vj d.; furs,
vj s.; faggots through the whole time, viij d.; sea-coal, vij d.; charcoal,
x d.; Paris candle; iiij d. ob.; xxviii pairs of gloves for the vicars
and masters of the schools; iij s. iv d. ob.; and for mending a silk
cope, ij d.

The bishop's great supper *on the eve of Innocents' day* cost xv s.
vj d. ob., viz.: in bread, vij d.; lord's bread, iv d.; ale, xxj d.; veal
and mutton, ix d. ob.; sausages, iv d.; two ducks, iv d.; twelve
chickens, ij s. vj d.; eight woodcocks and one plover, ijs. ijd.; three
dozen and ten field-fares, xix d.; small birds, iij d.; wine, ij s. iij d.;
various spices (or grocery), xj d.; sixty wardens (pears), v d. ob.;

----

* The meaning of "ad Novam" is uncertain.

honey, ij d. ob.; mustard, j d.; two pounds of candles, ij d. ob.; flour, ij d.; fuel, j d. ob.; and to the cook, vj d.

At the supper on *Innocent's day* was spent, in bread, iij d.; ale, v d.; veal and mutton, vij d.; pepper and saffron, j d.

In the next week nothing was done; but on Thursday, the 4th of January, being *the octave of Innocents' day*, they went to Kexby (seven miles from York), the mansion of Sir Thomas Utrecht, knight, who gave the bishop iij s. iv d. They returned to a supper, at which was spent, in bread, ij d.; ale, iv d.; and meat, v d. On the succeding Friday and Saturday the roll states that " they did not visit."

On the second Sunday of his episcopate, which was *the feast of Saint William* (Jan. 7), the bishop went out of town on his longest circuit. A girdle was now bought for him which cost iij d., and he had not gone far when his cap required mending at the expense of j d. His party took a breakfast before starting, and consumed, in bread, ij d.; in meat, v d.; and in ale, iij d. The sum of ij d. was also paid for " horse-bread." Their first visit appears to have been to the Prior of Kirkham, who gave the bishop ij s.; and the second to the wealthier Prior of Malton, whose offering was a noble. They proceeded next to the Countess of Northumberland living at Leconfield, who was the bishop's most generous benefactor: she gave him twenty shillings and a gold ring. From thence to Bridlington, where the prior gave him a noble. He next gathered iij s. iv d. from the Prior of Watton, and the like sum from the Rector of Baynton and from the Prior of Meaux. Between the two last places the cavalcade passed through Beverley, where a girth was bought for j d. He proceeded to Ferriby, where the prior gave him xx d.; Sir Stephen de Scrope gave him vj s. viij d.; and to the priory of Drax, where he received ij s.

On coming to the abbey of Selby, the head of that great monastery gave him a noble; from the Prior of Pontefract he had

half a noble; and from the Prior of St. Oswald at Nostell a noble.
The Prior of Monk Bretton gave him half a noble, and "Dominus
John Depdene" a noble. He went to the residence of the Lady
Marmion at Tanfield on the Yore and received a noble and a gold
ring with a silk purse; to the residence of Lady Darcy, "the Lady
of Harlsay," and obtained half a noble; and to the Lady Roos at
Helmsley Castle, who gave him a noble.

He now came to the abbey of Rievaulx and had only two shillings;
the like at Byland abbey; the like at Newburgh priory; and twenty
pence at the priory of Marton.

On the Saturday the travellers again returned to York, and had
a supper, for which the fish cost vj d , the bread ij d. ob., and the
ale ij d. The accompt of the "expenses within the city" concludes
with this item, "On the fifth Sunday and to the end of the Purifi-
cation (Feb. 2) nothing."

The expenses upon the road, which have not been hitherto
enumerated, were, in an offering at Bridlyngton, ij d., and given in
alms there j d. At that stage of the journey a new girth was
required, for which j d. was paid, and the old one was repaired for
an ob. A second horse-comb was also purchased, the first having
been bought at York, and the two together cost iiij d. Upon three
different occasions was money spent in "ferilay" = ferry-hire, or
payment at the ferry; the first time at Melsam, the second time at
Drax, and the third time at Harlsay. The charge at each place was
iiij d. At Selby they spent iiij d. in horse-bread, and paid a penny
to the barber, whose employment was more probably upon the
beard of the tenor singer or other men of the company than upon
the chin of the boy-bishop. The horses were re-shod at Ferriby,
at Fountains, and at Newburgh, costing in the first-named place
viij d., in the second iiij d., and in the third iij d.

The excursionists supped once at Leeds at a cost of xvij d. for themselves, and of xiij d. in hay and oats for the horses; and once at Ripley, where their own supper cost xvj d., and the hay and oats for the horses xij d. ob. In baiting at Allerton they spent vj d. and the like sum for horse-bread and hay at Helmslay. It may be noted that horse-bread is still in use in some parts of the continent. During the journey the boy-bishop alone seems to have been treated with wine, the cost of which was viij d.

The two last heads of the accompt enumerate the attendants upon the child-bishop. Under that of " Wages of servants and horses" it is stated that there was paid " To Nicholas de Newsome, his tenor singer, one mark; and to the same for his led horse, ij s.; to Robert Dawtry, his steward, one noble, and for his preachings in the chapel, ij s. j d. ob.; to John Baynton, chanting the medius voice part, x s.; to John Grene, v s.; to John Ellay, iij s. iv d.; to John Schapton, serving him with his two horses, x s. ij d.; to Thomas Marschale for one horse, iij s. iv d.; for a saddle for one horse, iij s. vj d.; to the baker for one horse, iij s. vj d.; and to Richard Fewler for two horses, v s. The " fees of the ministers serving in the church" were: To the succentor of the vicars, ij s.; to the sub-chancellor, xij d.; to the wax of the boys, xij d.; to the clerks of the vestments, xij d.; to the sacrists, xij d.; for the adornment of the episcopal chair, iv d.; in wood for stalls, iv d. (an entry which is obliterated); in common pence,[a] xviij d.; and to the guardian (or master) of the choristers, iij s. iv d.

The total sum of the expenses amounted to vj l. xiv s. x d. ob., and there consequently remained of the receipts, for the use of the bishop, forty shillings and sixpence halfpenny.[b]

York holds a conspicuous place in the annals of the boy-bishop. In the register of the capitulary acts of the Cathedral, under the

[a] Perhaps distributed to the choristers.
[b] A copy of the original document is given as an Appendix.

date Dec. 2, 1367, it is ordered, as an indispensable qualification, " that the Bishop of the boys should for the future be he who had served longest in the church, and who should be most suitable; provided, nevertheless, that he was sufficiently handsome in person; and that any election otherwise should not be valid.[a] The boy-bishop was supposed to be elected by his chapter, as were ordinary bishops; but the choice was probably directed by the higher authorities in favour of the most deserving boy.

Many other notices might possibly be found in the York records, but the search would be attended with some labour. A slight investigation made by Canon Raine, some few years since, revealed the following curious list of boy-bishops :—

Test. S. Nich.	6 Dec. 1416.	Confirm. elect.	Ric. Massam in Episc. puerorum.
„	6 Dec. 1417.	Conf.	„	Hen. Fournas.
„	6 Dec. 1418.	„	„	Thos. Thorp.
„	6 Dec. 1420.	„	„	—— de Burgh.
„	6 Dec. 1485.	„	„	Thos. Malson, choristæ.
„	6 Dec. 1486.	„	„	John Clerk, do.
„	6 Dec. 1487.	„	„	Thos. Greves, do.
„	6 Dec. 1488.	„	„	James Beswyk.
„	7 Dec. 1503.	• „	„	Ric. Plummer.
„	6 Dec. 1537.	„	„	Geo. Nevell, choristæ.

The election and investment of the boy-bishop certainly proceeded from the festival of sub-deacons, also called Festum Fatuorum, Festum Stultorum, Fête des Fous, Festival of Fools, &c.; the burlesque election of a mock pope, mock cardinals and bishops, attended by a thousand absurd ceremonies, gambols, and antics. "It does not appear," says Strutt, speaking of the former, "at what period this idle ceremony was first established, but probably it was ancient, at least we can trace it back to the

---

[a] Warton's *History of English Poetry*, ed. 1840, iii. 251, where other curious extracts from the York Registers are given.

fourteenth century [thirteenth century].ᵃ In all the collegiate
churches it was customary for one of the children of the choir,
completely apparelled in the episcopal vestments, with a mitre and
crosier, to bear the title and state of a bishop. He exacted a
ceremonial obedience from his fellows, who, dressed like priests,
took possession of the church, and performed all the ceremonies
and offices which might have been celebrated by a bishop and his
prebendaries. Warton, and the author of the MS. which he
has followed, add, 'the mass excepted'; but the proclamation of
Henry VIII. for the abolition of this custom, proves they did
' sing masse.' "ᵇ After the election of a boy-bishop, he was escorted
in his mitre by a solemn procession of the other boys to church,
where, as we have seen, he presided at the worship, and afterwards
he and his deacons went about singing from door to door, and
collecting money; not begging, but demanding it as a subsidy. In
1274 the Council of Nice prohibited this mock election, though
so late as the time of Hospinian, who wrote in the seventeenth
century, it was customary at schools dedicated to Pope Gregory the
Great, who was a patron of scholars, for one of the boys to be his
representative on the occasion and to act as pope, with some of his
companions as cardinals. As Brand wisely observes, 'Ecclesiastical
synods and censures have often proved too weak to suppress popular

ᵃ "On December 7, 1299, the morrow of St. Nicholas, the boy-bishop in the
chapel at Heton, near Newcastle-upon-Tyne, said vespers before Edward the First,
then on his way to Scotland, who gave a considerable present to him and the boys
that sang with him."—Hampson's *Medii Ævi Kalendarium*, i. 79. This is
possibly the earliest notice we have of the boy-bishop in this country. See also the
Wardrobe Account of 23 Edward I. 1299, published by the Society of Antiquaries,
p. 25.

ᵇ *Sports and Pastimes*, book iv. chap. 3, sect. 10. "Warton quotes the fragment
of a *computus* of Hyde Abbey, near Winchester, which is at variance with the
assertion, made by himself and Strutt, that the boy-bishop did not perform mass; it
is a disbursement, in 1327, for feasting the boy-bishop, who celebrated mass on St.
Nicholas's day."—Hampson, *Medii Ævi Kalendarium*, i. 80.

spectacles, which take deep root in the public manners, and are only concealed for a while, to spring up afresh with new vigour.'

The festival of the boy-bishop was largely aided by the contributions of the monastic establishments; to what extent may be gleaned from the following passage, extracted from a MS. note by Mr. Nichols. " In the yearly accompt rolls of the Priory of Finchale the *Episcopus Elemosinariæ* is first mentioned in the year 1367. For some years the money paid him is mixed with other sums; but in 1395 it stands alone as iij s. iiij d.; and again in 1413 (after having disappeared for some years), ' Item Episcopo Elemosinariæ ex curialitate, iij s. iiij d.;' that is, ' of courtesy,' and not absolutely of right; the same sum the next year; but in 1417 only ij s., and so for some years after. In 1423 the monks of Finchale, grown more generous, not only gave to the Bishop of the Almonry iij s., but also to the Bishop of Elvett, of courtesy, xx d. The latter must have been a boy-bishop elected in the parish, so called, an outlying portion of the city of Durham. In 1424 the Bishop of the Almonry again had iij s. iiij d., and so forward yearly until 1430; when again, and for several years after, the payment was only ij s. In 1439 the entry is, ' Et Episcopo Puerili Elemosinariæ, ij s.' which is repeated in subsequent years. In 1449 the entry is, ' Et in diversis donis datis hoc anno, ac Episcopo Puerili Dunelm. et cantoribus ad festum Natalis Domini, xij s. vj d.,' and so to 1457; but in 1458 the words ' ac Episcopo Puerili ' are carefully erased in both copies that exist of the roll, and the sum of the entry is reduced from xxvj s. to xxij s. This shows that the contribution was in that year withdrawn; nor was it again made until the year 1466, when the Episcopus Puerilis received iij s. iiij d. The same is returned in subsequent years with some intermissions. In 1474 the entry is, ' Et solvit ad officium Feretrarii (the keeper of the shrine of Saint Cuthbert at Durham) pro Episcopo Puerili, iij s. iiij d.'; and in 1478, ' Et ad

officium Feretrarii pro duobus annis Episcopo Puerili vjs. viijd.'
The payment of iiijs. iiijd. continues to the latest roll in 1528." *

Dr. George Hall, Bishop of Chester (who died in 1668), in his
" Triumph of Romanism" published in 1655, has a characteristic
passage concerning this festival: " What merry work," exclaims
the good bishop, " it was here in the days of our holy fathers (and
I know not whether, in some places, it may not be so still) that
upon St. Nicholas, St. Katherine, St. Clement, and Holy Innocents'
day, children were wont to be arrayed in chimera, rochets, surplices,
to counterfeit bishops and priests, and to be led, with songs and
dances, from house to house, blessing the people, who stood grinning
in the way to expect that ridiculous benediction ; yea, that boys in
that holy sport were wont to sing masses, and to climb into the
pulpit to preach (no doubt learnedly and edifying) to the simple

---

* Charters, &c. of Finchale Priory, *Surtees Soc.* 1837.

In his Glossary (p. ccccxxviii) Dr. Raine has inadvertently connected the
entries *Episcopo Puerili* with those *Cantoribus ad ludum suum*, adding that "in
later years, before the Reformation, the latter entry was the only one, but it referred
to both, and included the two constitutions." This, however, is not the case. The
entry *Episcopo Puerili*, iijs. iiijd. continues to the last, and more frequently than
otherwise separated by a considerable interval from the entry, *Cantoribus ad ludum
suum*, ijs: The Christmas *ludus* of the singing-men was clearly a distinct matter
from the celebration of the boy-bishop. It seems to have been simply a feast, like
the *Ludi Prioris*, to which the cell of Finchale yearly made a contribution
approaching or exceeding xxxs., and in 1483 a still larger sum, "Et in vino dato in
ludis domini Prioris et in die annalis Capituli, xxxviijs. ijd." From the similar
entry of xxxiiijs. in 1495, it appears that the Prior had yearly four of these *ludi*, of
which Dr. Raine has given various particulars in his Glossary *sub voce*, and which
are more fully developed in the Durham Household Book, another volume of the
Surtees Society, 1844. The false impression that these "games of the lord prior"
were connected with "the mock solemnity of the Boy Bishop" was carried on by
Dr. Raine from his early work on " Saint Cuthbert," 4to. 1838, p. 136, where he
also stated that the latter "was partly performed in the Infirmary, and always for its
benefit." These I believe to have been misapprehensions. The profits or surplus of
the collections made for the boy-bishop appear everywhere to have been given to the
boy himself.—J. G. N.

auditory. And this was so really done, that in the cathedral church of Salisbury (unless it be lately defaced) there is a perfect monument of one of these boy-bishops (who died in the time of his young pontificality) accoutred in his episcopal robes, still to be seen. A fashion that lasted until the later times of King Henry the Eighth, who, in 1541, by his solemn proclamation, printed by Thomas Berthelet, the King's printer, cum privilegio, stoutly. forbad the practice."[a]

The proclamation here alluded to was "devised by the Kings Majesty, by the advyse of his highness counsel, the xxii day of Julie, xxxiii Hen. VIII., commanding the feasts of Saint Luke, Saint Mark, Saint Mary Magdalene, Inuention of the Crosse, and Saint Lawrence, which had been vsed, should be nowe againe celebrated and kept holie days." And, following the example of the synod of Carnot, which in 1526 had decreed that no scholars, clerks, or priests should, under pretence of recreation, enact any folly or levity in the church on the feast of St. Nicholas, St. Catherine, the Innocents, or any other days, and that the garments of the fools performing theatrical characters should be cast out of church, Henry concludes his proclamation thus: "Whereas heretofore dyvers and many superstitions and chyldysh obséruances have be vsed, and yet to this day are observed and kept, in many and sundry parts of this realm, as vpon Saint Nicholas, Saint Catherine, Saint Clement, the Holy Innocents, and such like, children be strangelie decked and apparayled to counterfeit priestes, bishoppes, and women,[b] and so be ledde with songes and daunces from house to house, blessing the people and gatheryng of money;

[a] Quoted by Brand, *Pop. Antiq.* ed 1849, i. 422.

[b] In explanation of this we may remark that there is an injunction given to the Benedictine nunnery at Godstowe, in Oxfordshire, by Archbishop Peckham, in 1278, that on Innocents' day "the public prayers should not any more be said in the church of that monastery *per Parvulas*," *i.e.* little girls.

and boyes do singe masse and preache in the pulpitt, with svche other vnfittinge and inconuenient vsages, rather to the derysyon than any true glory of God, or honor of his sayntes: The Kynges Maiestie therefore, myndinge nothinge so moche as to aduance the true glory of God without vaine superstition, wylleth and commandeth that from henceforth all svch superstitious obseruations be left and clerely extinguished throwout his realmes and dominions, for asmvch as the same doth resemble rather the vnlawfull superstition of gentilitie, than the pure and sincere religion of Christe." [a]

In the second year of Queen Mary, when all the other ceremonies connected with the holidays of the saints had been revived, the festival of St. Nicholas was also resumed. Machyn tells us in his Diary, that on the 13th of November, 1554, it " was commanded by the Bishop of London (Bonner) to all clerks in the diocese of London to have Saint Nicholas, and to go abroad as many as could have it." On the 5th of December following, being the eve of the festival, this was counter-ordered; and " at the same time came a commandment (from what authority is not stated) that Saint Nicholas should not go abroad, nor about. But, notwithstanding, (adds Machyn) there went about Saint Nicholases in divers parishes, at St. Andrew's, Holborn, and St. Nicholas Olave, in Bread-street." [b]

Two years later the same writer notices the custom as fully re-established in the metropolis. " The 5th of December (1556) was Saint Nicholas' even, and Saint Nicholas went abroad in most parts of London singing after the old fashion, and was received with many good people into their houses, and had much cheer as ever they had in many places."

The following story, preserved in the Actes and Monuments of

---

[a] This proclamation is printed in Wilkins's *Concilia.*

[b] See the Diary of Henry Machyn, Citizen and Merchant Taylor of London, from A.D. 1550 to 1563. Edited by J. Gough Nichols, for the Camden Society, in 1848.

John Foxe, belongs to the same year. " A godly matrone, named Gertrude Crockhay, the wife of maistre Robert Crockehay, dwelling then at Saint Katharins by the Tower of London, abstained herself from the Popish church. She being in her husband's house, it happened in anno 1556 that the foolish Popish Saint Nicholas went about the parish, which she understanding shut her doores against him, and would not suffer him to come within her house. Then Doctor Mallet, hearing thereof (and being then maister of Saint Katherin's[a]) the next day came to her with xx. at his taile, thinking belike to fray her, and asked why she would not the night before let in Saint Nicholas, and receive his blessing, &c. To whom she answered thus, ' Sir, I knowe no Saint Nicholas (said she) that came hither.' ' Yes (quoth Mallet), here was one that represented Saint Nicholas.' ' In deede, Sir (saide she), here was one that is my neighboures childe, but not Saint Nicholas, for Saint Nicholas is in heaven. I was afraide of them that came with him to have had my purse cutte by them, for I have heard of men robbed by Saint Nicholas' clearkes,' &c. So Mallet, perceiving that nothing could be gotten at her hands, went his way as he came, and she for that time so escaped." [b]

" With the Catholic liturgy," says Warton, " all the pageantries of popery were restored to their ancient splendour by Queen Mary. Among others, the procession of the boy-bishop was too popular a mummery to be forgotten. In the preceding reign of Edward the Sixth, Hugh Rhodes, one of the Gentlemen of the Royal Chapel, published an English poem with the title " The Boke of Nurture, for men servants and children, or for the governaunce of youth, with *Stans puer ad Mensam*." In the following reign of

---

[a] From a subsequent passage it appears that Mrs. Crockhay's brother married Dr. Mallet's sister. Mallet became Dean of Lincoln.

[b] Foxe, edit. 1843-9, p. 1941.

Mary the same poet printed a poem consisting of thirty-six octave stanzas, entitled " The song of the Chyld-Bysshope, as it was songe before the Queenes Majestie in her privie chamber at her manour of Saynt James in the ffeeldes on Saynt Nicholas day and Innocents' day this yeare now present, by the Chylde-Bysshope of Poules churche with his company. Londini, in ædibus Johannis Cawood, typographi reginæ, 1555. Cum privilegio, &c." No copy of this curious poem is now known, although it is certain that Warton had seen it, for he thus describes it: " As to the song itself, it is a fulsome panegyric on the Queen's devotion, in which she is compared to Judith, Esther, the Queen of Sheba, and the Virgin Mary." [a]

The practice of electing a boy-bishop was common in colleges,[b] grammar-schools, and parish churches. As patron of scholars, St. Nicholas had a double feast at Eton College, where, in Catholic times, the scholars to avoid interfering, as it would seem, with the boy-bishop on St. Nicholas's day, elected their boy-bishop on St. Hugh's day, in November. Brand, indeed, was of opinion that the anniversary *Montem* of Eton is merely a corruption of the procession of the boy-bishop and his companions; the scholars, being prevented by the edict of Henry VIII. from continuing that ceremony, gave a new face to their festivity, and began their pastime at soldiers, and elected a captain. Even within the memory of persons living in 1777, when Brand wrote, the *Montem* was kept a little before Christmas, although subsequently held on Whit Tuesday.

" The boy-bishop had a set of pontificals provided for him. St.

---

[a] *History of English Poetry*, edit. 1840, iii. 265.

[b] At Magdalen College, Oxford, "on the eve of St. Nicholas, an entertainment at the expense of the College was served up to the choristers in the hall, at which the chaplains and clerks were also present, and occasionally the fellows. The boy-bishop was then chosen, and presented with gloves, &c. as marks of dignity, for which payments occur in the *libri computi* of the College."—Millard's *Historical Notices of the office of Choristers*, 1848, p. 50.

Paul's, London, had its 'una mitra alba cum flosculis breudatis—ad opus episcopi parvulorum—baculus ad usum episcopi parvulorum;' York Minster, too, its ' una capa de tissue pro episcopo puerorum; ' Lincoln Cathedral, a cope of red velvet, ordained for the barn-bishop; All Souls College, Oxford, 'j. chem (ches?) j. cap. et mitra pro episcopo Nicholao;' St. Mary's Church, Sandwich, 'a lytyll chesebyll for Seynt Nicholas bysschop.' For the boy-bishop's attendants capes were also made; and York had no fewer than ' novem capæ.pro pueris.' "[a]

Concerning vestments, jewels, &c., used by the boy-bishop and his companions, we have many curious notices handed down to us, some few of which we have placed together.

A parchment roll of the fifteenth century, printed in the notes to the Northumberland Household Book, gives us the following inventory.

"*Contenta de Ornamentis Episcopi Puerorum.*

" Imprimis, i myter, well garneshed with perle and precious stones, with nowches of silver, and gilt before and behind.

" Item, iiij rynges of silver and gilt, with four redde precious stones in them.

" Item, i pontifical with silver and gilt, with a blew stone in hytt.

" Item, i owche broken, silver and gilt, with iiij precius stones, and a perle in the myddes.

" Item, a crosse, with a staf of coper and gilt, with the ymage of St. Nicolas in the myddes.

" Item, i vesture, redde, with lyons of silver, with brydds [birds] of gold in the orferes [borders] of the same.

" Item, i albe to the same with starres in the paro.

---

[a] Dr. Rock's *Church of our Fathers*, iii. part ii. p. 217, where authorities are quoted.

" Item, i white cope, stayned with tristells and orferes [of]
redde sylkes, with does of gold, and whytt napkins about ther
necks.

" Item, iiij copes [of] blue sylk, with red orferes, trayled with
whitt braunchis and flowres.

" Item, i steyned cloth of the ymage of St. Nycholas.

" Item, i tabard of skarlet, and a hodde thereto, lyned with whitt
sylk.

" Item, a hode of skarlett, lyned with blue sylk."

In the will of Thomas Rotheram, Archbishop of York, dated
in 1481, is a bequest to the College of that place of a mitre
of cloth of gold with two silver enamelled " knoppes" to be
worn by the " *Barnes-Bishop*." This is, perhaps, the same
mitre which is named in the inventory of jewels and valuables
belonging to the Cathedral of York, in Dugdale's Monasticon.
—"Item una Mitra parva cum *Petris* pro Episcopo Puerorum." The tarnished silver knobs seem to have been mistaken
for stones.[a]

In a MS. inventory of vestments, &c., committed to the care of
the Sacristan of Magdalen College, Oxford, in 1495, are, " *pro
pueris*," tunicles, red and white and crimson, with orfreys [borders]
of damask and velvet, one set of albs of blue damask, and two with
apparels of red silk ; and, lastly, a banner of St. Nicholas, the
patron of children.[b]

In the Churchwardens' Accounts of St. Mary-at-Hill, London,
10 Henry VI., mention is made of " two children's copes, also a
myter of cloth of gold set with stones." Under 1549 we have in
the same accounts, " For 12 oz. silver, being clasps of books and the

[a] Hampson's *Medii Ævi Kalendarium*, i. 80. See also Hearne's *Liber Niger Scaccarii*, 1728, ii. 674, 686.

[b] Millard's *Historical Notices of the office of Choristers*, 1848, p. 49.

CAMD SOC. *d*

bishop's mitre, at v s. viij d. per oz., vj l. xvj s. j d." These last were sold. In the Inventory of Church Goods belonging to the same parish, at the same time, we have, " Item, a mitre for a bishop at St. Nicholas-tyde, garnished with silver and aneyld, and perle and counterfeit stone." Another extract from the same accounts, in 1554, has this entry, " Paid for makying the bishop's myter, with stuff and lace that went to it, iij s. Paid for a boke for Nicholas, viij d." This was the restoration of the ceremony under Queen Mary.[a]

Among the inventories of Westminster Abbey [b] is "The vj myter of Seynt Nycholas bysshoppe, the grounde therof of whyte sylk, garnysshed complete with ffloures, gret and small, of sylver and gylte, and stones complete in them, with the scripture, Ora pro nobis Sancte Nicholai, embrodered theron in perll, the sydes sylver and gylt, and the toppys of sylver and gylt, and enamelyd with ij labelles of the same, and garnysshed in lyk maner, and with viij long bells of sylver and gylt, weying all together xxiij unces." And among the kanapys is the following, " a gret blewe clothe with Kyngs on horsse-bake for Saynt Nicholas cheyre." [c]

The question of money struck for the boy-bishop — " St. Nicholas' pence "—is thus summed up in a MS. note by Mr. Nichols: " The only place in this country where I have detected any evidences of such imitative coinage is Bury St. Edmund's. In the church of St. Mary in that town there was a Guild of St. Nicholas; and in the years 1842-3, during the removal of the priests' stalls from the chancel-aisles to the choir of that church, a number of leaden pieces, formed in imitation of money, were discovered. Some were published in the Numismatic Chronicle, and others in the Journal of the Archæological Association; and

[a] Brand's *Popular Antiquities*, i. 424, edit. 1849, where authorities are quoted.
[b] London and Middlesex Arch. Soc. iv. 318.   [c] Ibid. 328.

as many as a dozen varieties, some of the size of groats and others of pennies, are described in ' An Architectural and Historical Account of the Church of St. Mary, Bury St. Edmund's. By Samuel Tymms, F.S.A., 1854.' 4to. pp. 62—67. Mr. Roach Smith was disposed to regard these tokens as 'medals of presence,' struck to be given to those who at particular seasons assisted at particular services; but Mr. Daniel H. Haigh thought they were undoubtedly relics commemorative of the solemnity of the boy-bishop. He remarked that they were evident imitations of the groats and pennies of Henry VII. and his predecessors; and, as the coinage of St. Edmundsbury did not differ from that of the royal mints, they may be presumed to have followed the general type of the Bury coinage. He adds the following reasons for their not possessing the variety of devices which marks the continental *monnaies des Evêques des Innocens.*

" The money of the Archbishops of Canterbury and York, the Bishop of Durham, and the Abbot of Reading, was distinguished from that of our Edwards, Henries, and Richards, by a simple mint-mark only. The Abbot of St. Edmundsbury, in imitation of whose right of coinage these tokens were probably issued, is not known to have placed any distinguishing mark upon his coins. In France, where almost every prelate and baron was allowed to strike money in his own name, we find the names of the Bishops of Innocents, and of Fools, similarly commemorated upon their pseudo-coinage. In England, on the contrary, where all the current coin of the realm was impressed with 'the image and superscription' of the reigning King, and where also the ceremony of the boy-bishop was more exclusively a religious ceremony, the name of St. Nicholas appears on the tokens issued in commemoration of this festival, and that of the infant prelate is lost.

" It was possibly the practice to sink a new die each year for this coinage, which will account for the varieties of type that are found; and it may have been from design, rather than accident, that some were thrown behind the stalls of the church.

" There are, however, other similar tokens, which we can scarcely appropriate to the festival of the boy-bishop, though they may have been struck for other festivals of a similar character. One bears a mitred head between the letters s and m, with the legend SANCTE MARTINE ORA PRO, and on the reverse a shield charged with a chevron between them, and the legend GRATIA DEI SVM ADSVM. See also in Rigollot's work, p. 96, SANCTE AUGUSTINE ORA PRO NOBIS.

" With respect to Mr. Roach Smith's suggestion that these were commemorative ' medals of presence,' it is to be remembered that the pilgrims' tokens, of which so many have been recovered in recent reseaches, were usually fastened on the cap or garment, and only figured on one side. These tokens, on the contrary, are evidently struck in imitation of money, and were, therefore, probably intended to be so regarded, at least in sport."

As regards the diminutive effigy in Salisbury Cathedral (mentioned by Gregory and Hall), there is considerable doubt as to its being to the memory of a boy-bishop. The following note by the late Mr. J. G. Nichols is interesting, and throws some light upon this obscure subject. " In the third volume of the Archæological Journal, 1846, will be found an essay, by W. S. Walford, Esq., F.S.A., on ' The cross-legged effigy at Horsted Keynes, Sussex; with some remarks on early effigies of diminutive dimensions.' Mr. Walford remarks (p. 237), that ' Diminutive effigies, in which the proportions are those of a man, are sometimes supposed to represent children, but I think without good reason. An effigy is, *prima facie*, to be considered as representing that, to which, having a regard to the costume and general appearance, it bears most resemblance, irrespectively of its size; for it is unreasonable from size alone to infer that it was intended for a full-grown person. Thus, a small effigy, apparently of a knight or priest, is to be taken as representing an adult; for till a certain age knighthood and priests' orders were not usually conferred; and we have no reason *a priori* to expect to meet with an effigy of a child attired as a knight or priest.' Mr. Walford afterwards adds, ' The story of the boy-bishop at Salisbury Cathedral needs confirmation.'

" In many cases there is no doubt the diminutive effigy was placed *where the heart of the deceased was deposited*, and one of the full size where the body was interred. Indeed it is not improbable that this may have been the meaning of all such diminutive effigies; for Mr. Walford further states ' I have not been able to meet with any well-authenticated case of a diminutive effigy placed over the grave of an adult.' But there are ascertained cases of such effigies commemorating the interment of a heart; of which the following may be particularised:

" Blanche (d'Artois) dowager Queen of Navarre, wife of Edmond Earl of Lancaster (ob. 1302), a figure two feet long, now in the Cathedral of St. Denis, brought from the conventual church of the minoresses at Nogent l'Artault in Champagne, founded by her; her body being buried in Paris."

" At Tenbury in Gloucestershire, a cross-legged effigy in mailed armour, four feet long, holding a heart ."

" At Ayot St. Lawrence, Herts, effigy two feet three inches long, also formerly holding a heart, now broken.

" I may also mention a small effigy holding a heart which my father bought in 1842 from the garden of the lodge in the Green Park, Westminster, when that house was removed (its original locality not ascertained), and which after his death I gave to the British Museum."

The two sermons following this Introduction are perhaps the sole
existing relics in the English language of a species of literary
composition once as familiar as our own annual sermons for benefit
clubs, or those for the sons of the clergy.   At a time when preaching
was rare, except in large churches, the sermon delivered by the
boy-bishop on the Feast of the Holy Innocents, commonly called
Childermas day, was one of regular rotation, and countenanced by
due authority.   Modern writers have usually regarded the festival
of this personage, and all his proceedings, as a mere revel or
mummery, without any redeeming features.   The contemporary
sentiment upon the subject was apparently otherwise.   The ancient
custom was not only allowed and continued by the founders of
Winchester and Eton, but when Dean Colet dictated the laws
for his grammar-school, in the year 1512, he directed that his
scholars should on every Childermas day hear the child-bishop's
sermon in Paul's, and afterwards, attending the high mass, offer,
each of them, one penny to the child-bishop.[a]

Commenting upon this, Warton, in his History of English
Poetry, considered it "surprising that Colet, Dean of St. Paul's, a
friend to the purity of religion, and who had the good sense and
resolution to censure the superstitions and fopperies of Popery in
his public sermons, should countenance this idle farce of the boy-
bishop in the statutes of his school at St. Paul's, which he founded
with the view of establishing the education of youth on a more
rational and liberal plan than had yet been known."

[a] "All these children shall every Childermas daye come to Paull's churche, and
here the childe-bishoppes sermon, and after be at highe masse, so each of them offre
a j d. to the childe-bishopp, and with the maisters and surveyours of the scoole.   In
generall processions, when they be warnyde, theye shall go tweyne and tweyne
togither soberly, and not synge oute, but saye devoutly, tweyne and tweyne, vij
salmes wit latynye."—MS. copy of the Statutes of St. Paul's School, Additional
MS. No. 6274, Brit. Mus.

To all that can be said in the praise of Colet there are few that will be inclined to object. As the greatest friend upon English soil of the greatest foreigner that visited England in his time, the Dean of St. Paul's is emphatically the *laudatus a laudate.*ᵃ Acknowledging then both his piety and his good sense, it is only reasonable to conclude that, after having occupied the Deanery of St. Paul's for seven years, Colet had deliberately formed an opinion in favour of the boy-bishop's sermon, as being productive of certain beneficial effects upon its hearers; at any rate as a means of turning to some good account the proceedings of a festival of which the remainder was devoted to pageantry, revelry, and the collection of a tax upon the charity and good nature of the community.

We may conclude that the Church in this matter, as in so many others in which she had to withstand the inveterate habits and propensities of human nature, endeavoured to control and modify doings which she could not utterly prohibit or abolish. In limiting the revelry of clerks and ecclesiastics to the younger members, or at least to giving to the children the apparent conduct and management of the sports most allowable to their period of life, one attempted to set bounds to a festivity, which with those of greater growth was apt to run into vicious excess; and by the collation or sermon, which she placed in the mouth of the boy-bishop, it was her aim to season the indulgence with some ingredients of instruction and admonition.

The sermon at St. Paul's appears to have been usually prepared by the almoner of that church; and the same practice was probably established elswhere.ᵇ William de Tolleshunte, almoner of St.

ᵃ The great foreigner was of course Erasmus. A sermon from his pen, " Concio de puero Jesu," spoken by a boy of St. Paul's School, is still extant. It is printed in the Rotterdam edition of Erasmus's works, folio, 1704.

ᵇ Brayley rightly conjectures, as to the "chylde-byshop's sermons," that "probably these orations, though affectedly childish, were composed by the more aged members of the Church."—London and Middlesex, ii. 229.

Paul's, in his will, made in 1329, bequeathed several books to remain in the almonry for ever, "all the quires of sermons of the Feasts of the Holy Innocents which the boy-bishops were wont to preach in my time." These have probably long since perished, nor have we heard of any similar productions being extant among the manuscripts of our cathedral churches.

It would be no difficult task to enumerate the names of many eminent men who commenced life as choristers. Among popes we have Sergius I., Sergius II., Gregory II., Stephen III., and Paul I.; among English saints, Wulstan, Bishop of Peterborough; among the first choir of Durham, Eata, Bishop of Lindisfarn; and from the choristers of Magdalen College, Oxford (of whom a nearly perfect list is preserved from 1546 to the present time), four bishops: Cooper, Bickley, Nicholson, and Hopkins; Pierce, afterwards President of the College; and Archdeacon Todd, the editor of Milton.[a] After all something may be said in favour of the custom we have endeavoured to describe. And, perhaps, Strype was not far wrong when he concludes " that it gave a spirit to the children, and the hopes that they might one time or other attain to the real mitre made them mind their books." The spirit of emulation has always had a beneficial effect upon youth. Let us look then kindly upon that ancient ceremony which has been denounced as "the foolish mummery of ignorant monks."

[a] See the Rev. J. E. Millard's *Historical Notices of the office of Choristers.* 12mo. 1848.

TWO SERMONS

PREACHED BY

THE BOY BISHOP.

PREFACE.

Only two sermons in English preached by boy-bishops have been discovered, which follow in this volume. The former of these sermons was printed at least twice, shortly after its composition, but only one copy of each edition is known to be still in existence.

The earlier is from the press of Wynkyn de Worde, and has at the end the device of his master, Caxton. This was unknown to Ames and Herbert, but is described in Dr. Dibdin's *Typographical Antiquities*, ii. 379, from the copy which belonged to Richard Heber. It appears in the sale catalogue of the Heber Library, Part vi., lot 567, and is now reprinted from the same exemplar, through the kindness of the Rev. J. Fuller Russell, its present possessor.

The title consists of only these two lines placed at the head of a blank page—

En die Innocencium Sermo pro Episcopo puerorum.

The whole tract comprises twelve leaves, of which the second, third, and fourth, have the signatures a ij, a iij, a iiij; and the seventh, eighth, ninth, and tenth, b, b ij, b iij, b iiij. On the reverse of this last signature the sermon ends; and a list of the indulgences of Pope John XXII. succeeds. These occupy the remainder of two pages and a half. A leaf with the print of the Crucifixion—the same as given by Caxton in the *Golden Legend*, 1493—concludes the tract.

According to Dr. Dibdin this sermon "must have been printed before the year 1496, as the soul of Bishop Kemp is prayed for in it, who died in 1489; and his successor Hill in 1495 or 1496."

The second copy of this sermon, preserved in the Library of the British Museum, has no printer's name or date, but it is evidently subsequent to the time of Wynkyn de Worde. It has no variation except differences of spelling, which are as numerous as is often found in black-letter chronicles and other books of that era. On the whole, the earlier edition, according to Mr. Nichols, is to be preferred. Typographical misprints occur in both editions, particularly in the Latin. These the Editor has silently corrected.

The second sermon is now printed for the first time. It is from the Cotton MS. Vespasian A. xxv. in the British Museum. It was written in 1558, and preached in Gloucester Cathedral in the same year. Of the author, Richard Ramsey, we know but little. From Wood's *Fasti* (edit. Bliss, i. 110), we learn that Richard Ramsey was admitted Bachelor in Divinity in 1539. He furthermore says " Richard Hallyny, *alias* Ramsey, S.T.P., was admitted Vicar of Wellan in Somersetshire, 1546, and had one or more dignities in the church;" one of these dignities being, according to Archdeacon Furney, the sixth prebendal stall at Gloucester. Fosbroke (*History of Gloucester*, p. 114) tells us that Richard Ramsey, *alias* Hawley, M.A., was installed Rector of Shenington, co. Gloucester, in 1555, and was deprived in 1559." It is clear from the sermon that the author was of the old religion.

Of John Stubs, " Querester "—the boy-bishop who " pronounced " the sermon—we know nothing. It has been conjectured that he was John Stubbes, the author of " The Discoverie of a Gaping Gulff," who suffered the loss of his right hand in 1579 for his seditious writings; but this is unlikely. This old worthy was born in or about 1543, and matriculated as a pensioner of Trinity College, Cambridge, November 12, 1555, being then of immature age. The John Stubs who delivered the boy-bishop's sermon in Gloucester Cathedral in 1558 has yet to be identified.

EDWARD F. RIMBAULT.

IN DIE INNOCENCIUM
SERMO PRO EPISCOPO PUERORUM.

Laudate Pueri Dominum.

PSALMO CENTESIMO XII° et pro hujus collacionis fundamento.

" PRAYSE ye childerne almyghty God," as the Phylosophre* sayth
in dyverse places. All those thynges that have the habyte of parfyght
cognycyon may move themself and conveye themself to theyr ende,
as a beest havynge sensyble knowlege, and man more parfyghter,
bothe sensyble and intellygyble, may move themself whether they
wyll, and so conveye al theyr accyons and dedes to theyr naturall ende;
but *carencia cognicione,* those thynges that lacke cognycyon, have no
mocyon of themself, nother be dyrected to theyr ende without the
helpe of an other. As an arowe of hymself can not be movyd ne
dyrected unto the prycke without the redy conveyaunce of hym that
shoteth, thrugh whom dyrectly he attayneth his ende and is shotte
to the prycke.

In as moche thenne as mankynde is ordeyned unto an ende ferre
excedynge the lymytes of nature, as it is wryten by the Holy Ghost
in Ysay lxiiij°, *Oculus non vidit, Deus, absque te quæ preparasti exspec-
tantibus te;* et prima ad Corintheos secundo — *Oculus non vidit, nec
aures audivit, nec in cor hominis ascendit quæ preparavit Deus dili-
gentibus illum.* " The eye of a man hath not seen, nother his eeres
herde, nother it can not be thought in his herte, thende that Almyghty God hath ordened for them that lovyth hym." To this ende
man, havynge the use of reason and parfyte knowlege, is dyrected

---

* *Qu. an error for the Psalmist?*

by his free wyll as by a pryncypall in hymself to move hym to God.
And also by fayth as a pryncypall above naturall knowlege, without
the whiche it is impossyble to plese God and attayne to the ende of
grace in this present lyf and glory in heven, as it is wreten, *Sine fide
impossibile est placere Deo.* Whyle it is so that man endowed with
use of reason, havynge naturall knowlege and free, maye not suffy-
cyently dyrect hymself to the ende that God hath ordeyned to without
the helpe of fayth, as it is wryten, Jheremiæ iiijº, *Non est enim hominis
vincere, neque viri est ut ambuleter et dirigat gressus ejus.* It is not in
mannes power for to overcome vyce of hymself, nother for to walke
parfyghtly and dyrecte his gooynge in the lawe of God, but by his
grace assystente. Moche more those that bene chylderne for tender-
nesse of age and lacke of knowlege can not dyrect theyr dedes con-

[Children
newly set to
school.]

venyently to that ende without specyall helpe of God. In token
herof childerne newely sette to scole, lackynge the use of reason and
the habyte of cognycyon, have a recourse to Goddes dyreccyon,
fyrste lernynge this (*Cristis Crosse be my spede*), and so begynnyth

[The A. B. C.]

the A B. C. In wytnesse of defawte of this perfeccion in knowlege,
Pyctagoras, to the dyreccyon of Chylderne, he founde fyrste this letter

[The letter Y.]

in the A. B. C. ɥ, the whyche as Ysider [a] sayth *Ethimologis* is formyd
and made after the symylytude of mannes lyfe, for this letter ɥ is
made of two lynes; one is a right lyne, the other is half ryght and

[Infancy.]

half crokyd. And soo verely the Infant age of a childe is ryght
neyther dysposed to vertue neyther to vyce, as the Phylosophre sayth,
Tanquam tabula nuda in qua nichil depingitur. But the seconde age

[Adolescence.]

is called *Adolescencia*, and hath two lynes, a ryght and a crokyd, sygne-
fyenge the dysposycion that he hath thenne to vyce and thenne to vertue. In the whiche age is the brekynge of every chylde to goodnes or
to lewdenes. Therfore that age is moost uncertayn in knowlege, as
Salomon sayth, Proverbior. xxxº, *Tria sunt michi difficilia ad. cognos-
cendum, et quartum penitus ignoro. Viam navis in medio maris, et
viam viri in adolescencia.* " Thre thynges (sayth Salomon) bene

---

[a] Originum, sive Ethymologiarum libri xx., one of the works of Saint Isidorus Hispa-
lensis, bishop of Seville, 601—636.

harde to me to knowe, and the fourth utterly I knowe not. The
flyghte of the egle in the ayer; The waye of the serpent on the
erthe;[a] The sayllyng of a shyppe in the see; But the fourth and moost
hardest is to understande the waye of a man in his growynge age."
Tho children thenne the whiche lacke dyscrecyon, use of reason,
and parfyght cognycyon, and yet attayne to the ende that is prepared
for mannes blysse, as thyse blessyd Innocentes whoos solempnyte [The Inno-
we halowe this daye (*Qui non loquendo sed moriendo confessi sunt*) cents.]
may moost in a specyall laude that gloryous Lorde (*sequentes Agnum
quocumque ierit,*) to whom by our Moder Holy Chirche in tytle of
tryumphe may contynually be applyed the wordes of my tyme [b]
(*Laudate, pueri, Dominum*), ye chosen chylderne of God, lackynge
the use of cognycyon and yet gloryfyed by your passyon in lyfe
everlastynge, prayse ye God.

In the begynnynge thenne of this symple exhortacyon, that I a
chylde, wantynge the habyte of connynge, maye be dyrected by hym
that gave to that childe Danyell *Sermonem rectum et Spiritum
Deorum,* somwhat to say to his laude and praysynge, and to alle
pure chylderne that bene here present edifyenge, we shall atte this
tyme devoutly make our prayers.

In the whiche prayers I recommende unto your devocyons the [Bidding
welfare of all Chrysts chirche; our holy fader the Pope with alle Prayer.]
the Clergye, my Lorde of Caunterbury, and the ryghte reverende
fader and worshypfull lorde my broder Bysshopp of London your dyo-
cesan, also for my worshypfull broder [the] Deane of this cathedrall
chirche, wytn all resydensaryes and prebendaryes of the same. And
moost intyerly I praye you to have myself in your specyal devocyon,
so that I may contynue in this degree that I now stande, and never
more herafter to be vexed with Jerom's vysyon, the whiche is wryten
Jeremiæ primo: whan the good Lorde askyd of Jeremye, *Quid tu* [Jeremiah's
vides, Jeremia? he answered and sayd *Virgam vigilantem ego video,* waking rod.]
" A waken rodde I see," sayd Jeremye. Truely thys waken rodde
oftentymes hath troubled me in my childehode, that *lambi mei im-*

---

[a] These two clauses are deficient in the Latin.   [b] *i. e.* theme (or text).

pleti sunt illusionibus, et non est sanitas in carne mea; afflictus sum et humiliatus sum nimis. And therfor, though I be now in hye dygnyte, yet whan I see other here my mayster that was thenne, *operuit confusio faciem meam; a voce contremuerunt labia mea.* As Nero the Emperour wold to his mayster Seneca,[a] the same wysshe I wold to my mayster I love soo well. And for theyr true dylygence that all my maysters the whiche taughte me ony connynge in my youthe gave to me, I wolde they were promytted [b] to be perpetuall felowes and collegeners of that famouse college of the Kynges foundacyon in Southwerke that men calle the Kynges Benche. Gretter worshypp I cannot wysshe than for to sytte in the Kynges owne Benche. And for by cause charyte is parfyght yf it be extendyd as well to the ende of the lyf as it is the lyf self, I wolde they sholde ende ther lyf in that holy waye the whyche often tymes I radde whan that I was Querester, in the Marteloge of Poules, where many holy bodyes deyed, callyd in Latyn *Via Tiburtina :* in Englysshe asmoche to saye as the highe waye to Tyburne. In this behalf ye shall praye specyally for all prelates that cometh to theyr dygnytee as I dyde; for, thanked be God, wythout conspyracy, lordshyp, or symony I was sette in thys degree; for verely promocyon in ony realme hadde *per demonum Simonem et principem* [c] hath and shall brynge Crystys chirche *in confusionem dampnabilem.*

In the seconde partye ye shall praye for the wele and peas of all Crysten reames, specyally for the reame of Englonde, Our soverayne lorde the Kyng, Our soverayne lady the Quene, My lorde the Prynce, My lady the Kynges Moder, My lorde her Husbonde, with all the Lordes of the Realme; The welfare of this Cyte, for my ryght worshypful broder and lover the Mayer, with all the Aldermen and Shyrefs.

In the thyrde partye, all the soules lyenge in the paynes of Purgatory ; specyally for the soule of the reverende fader my

[The King's Bench.]

[The highway to Tyburn.]

[He was preferred without conspiracy, lordship, or simony.]

[Souls in purgatory.]

---

[a] That he should make away with himself. This and the following passages are confirmatory of other accounts that we have of the severe discipline then exercised in schools.
[b] *i.e.* promoted.   [c] So in the original.

lorde Thomas Kempe late Bysshop, and for the soules of all Bene- [Bishop
factours of thys chirche of Poules, wyth all Crysten soules, for the Kempe].
whiche and for the entent premysed I praye you devoutly saye a
Pater Noster and an Ave.

Laudate Pueri Dominum (ut supra).

In as moche as Cryste sayth in the Gospell, *Sinite parvulos venire
ad me, quia talium est regnum Celorum* (Mathei xix°.) " Suffre ye
childerne to come to me, for of suche the kyngdom of heven is
fulfylled," by whom, after saynt Austyn (*in originali, ubi thema*),[a]
it is not oonly understonde those that bene chylderne of age, but
those that bene chylderne pure in clennesse from synne and malyce.
As the holy appostle saynt Poule sayth, *Nolite effici pueri sensibus,
malicia autem parvuli estote* (prima ad Corintheos xiiij°) " Be ye not
chylderne in your wyttes; but from all synne and malyce be ye
chylderne in clennesse." And in this fourme alle maner of people
and al maner of ages in clennesse of lyf ought to be pure as
childerne, to whom generally may I saye *Laudate, pueri, Dominum;
Laudate, pueri, Dominum in infantia; laudate Dominum in adole-
scentia; laudate Dominum in perseverante etate humana,*—"Prayse,
ye childerne, your God in your infant age; Prayse ye hym in your
growynge age; And prayse ye hym perseverauntly *(usque in senco
tum et senium)* in your mannes age." And in thyse thre praysynge
of thre ages shall stande the processe of this symple Collacyon.

Thyse thre ages after the consceyte of the appostle *(ad Galathas* [Three ages
and *ad Romanos)* is lykened to the thre lawes,—that is to saye— likened to the
to the Lawe of Kynde, the Lawe Wryten, and the Lawe of Grace. thre Laws.]
The first age is likenyd unto the Lawe of Kynde. A childe fyrste [Infancy to the
whan he is in his infant age is not constreyned unto no lawes; Law of Kind.]
he is not corrected nother beten; and there is no defaute layde
unto hym, but utterly he is lefte unto the lawe of kynde. Do he
what somever he wyll, no man doth blame hym. Morally the state
of man inmedyatly after synne was verely the state of childehode

---

[a] A reference to Saint Augustine's Commentary on the Gospel of St. Matthew, where
the text (*thema*) occurs.

and infans havinge no nouryce. Whan that man was utterly left without ony expressyd lawe, havynge no mayster, to his owne naturall inclynacyon as to his lawe, there was no lawe of God newe put to hym. Many defawtes dyde he, and to many inconvenyences he ranne. Correccyon was there none, but utter destruccyon, as Noes floode, destroyenge all infantes of mankynde save viij. persones (*Genesis* vij°.) The destruccyon of Sodome and of Gomor with other cytees (*Genesis* xix°.) And lyke wyse as a childe, havynge noo nouryce nor guyder deputed to hym, may as well renne in to the fyre or water as to go besyde, soo verely in the fyrste age of man, in the lawe of kynde, a man beynge wythout a nouryce or guyder, lefte to hys naturall guydynge, mysusyd soo ferre hymselfe, that he ranne to water where he was utterly destroyed as I sayde before, save Noes housholde, and also to the fyre, where a grete parte was destroyed. And verely, Maysters, yf we clerely consydre our lyf and state that we stande in now in thyse dayes, I fere me we shall fynde ourself soo ferre guyded by our sensuall nature, that we shall nede to be purefyed to our streyte correccyon wyth a streyte afflyccyon, as [Negligence of Spiritual rulers.] the water or the fyre. And all for lacke of our maysters and nouryces all wrapped in neclygence taketh none attendaunce to us. Our maysters and nouryces spyrytuall, *Querentes quæ sua sunt et non quæ Jhesu Christi, sunt canes muti non valentes latrare* (Ysaye lvi°.) [And of Temporal.] Our temporall rulers *Infideles, socii furum, diligunt munera, sequuntur retribuciones ; pupillo non judicant, causa viduæ non ingreditur ad eos.* (Ysaye i°.) This neclygence in our nouryces spyrytuall and temporall causeth in the Chirche insolent lyf, seculer conversacyon (*In habitu interiori et exteriori, ut qualis populus talis sit et* [Prevalent sins.] *sacerdos.*) In the temporalte it causeth that manslaughter is not sette by; lechery is pleysure; robbery and dysceyte is called chevesaunce; extorcyon lordshyp, power; falshede, a fete of wytte; usury counted no synne. *Quomodo facta est meretrix civitas fidelis, plena judicii. Justicia habitavit in ea, nunc autem homicidæ. Argentum tuum versum est in scoriam. Vinum tuum mixtum est aqua.* (Ysaye i°.) A merveyllous chaunge! somtyme our reame was prosperous,

now it is in mysery; somtyme Ryghtwysnesse was the cheyf ruler,
now Falshede is quarter-mayster; somtyme was inhabytaunt Peas,
Love, and Charyte, now Wrathe and Manslaughter and false Dyssymu-
lacyon; somtyme Trouth was mayster of our marchauntes, (*nunc vero
usura et dolus*). And somtyme Trouth stode upryght, now he is fallen. [The fall of
Good men have inserchyd the strete where he felle; some sayde he Truth.]
fell in Lombarde Strete, some sayde in Buklarsbury. And whan it [Lombard
was utterly knowe he was fallen in every strete (*Veritas corruit in* Street;
Bucklers-
plateis), the cause is none other but we lacke our maysters and bury.]
guyders that sholde streytly attende in this Infant age of condycyon
that we bene in.

Whan that infant age is ended, the fader provydeth for hys
childe for a mayster, the whyche gyveth instruccyon in small
doctrynes, as in hys Donate, Partes of reason, and suche other,[a] the
whiche mayster comunely is called *Pedagogus* in Latyne. This
mayster gevyth commaundementes to the childe in his growynge
age. And he breke them he is sharpely correctyd. There is no [Punishments
fawte that he doth but he is punysshed. Somtyme he wryngeth of the schoolmaster.]
hym by the eeres. Sometyme he geveth hym a strype on the honde
wyth the ferell. Some tyme beteth hym sharpelywith the rodde.
And so with commaundementes and sharpe correccyon he geveth
hym full instruccyon in the lawer scyence.[b] So in lyke manere
after the lawe of kynde. As mankynde grewe in age almyghty
God provyded to man an enformer[c] that was called Moyses, the [Moses.]
whiche sholde teche man his pryncypalles and small and rude
doctrynes. And so the olde lawe taught to man his Donate and
Partes of reason. Also he taught hym how he sholde gyve to God his
partes: the whyche were sacrefyces, oblacyons and tythes justely and [Tithes, &c.]
truely to be gyven to God—as it is wryten Ecclesiasticis xxxv°.) *Da
Altissimo secundum Donatum ejus.* That what thou sholdest gyve

---

[a] The Grammar of Ælias Donatus was one of the earliest books placed in the hands
of boys.

[b] The lower sciences.

[c] *Informator* was a usual Latin word for a schoolmaster.

[Alms.] also to thy neyghbour and broder his partes, that is to saye, almes dedes frely wythout grutchynge, lenynge ᵃ of thy good without ony trust or hope of usury, and forgevynge thy neyghbour yf he be in necessyte without trouble for Goddes sake; and lyke wyse as the people under Moyses growynge in childehode, thyse thynges were taught by the whiche specyally Goddes lawe and praysynge was encreaced, so in our growyng age in vertue that gode Lorde (*cujus laus est in ecclesia sanctorum*) canne not be better praysed, than yf we gyve unto hym justly and truely his Donat, to hym oblacyons, sacrefyces, and tythes. To our neyghbour mercyfully geve oure almesse, and pyteuously forgyve offences and dettes to theym that bene nedy and maye not paye. Thyse bene the thynges that longeth to Goddes praysynge in mankyndes childehode, as is wryten of Thoby (Thobie primo,) *Hæc et his similia puerulus secundum legem* [Severity of the *observabat.* In Moyses tyme streyte commaundementes were gyven law of Moses.] to Man, streyte punysshmentes and sharpe correccyons; they were taken by the eere streytly, whan it commaunded in the Lawe *aurem pro aure, dentem pro dente*, without ony mercy. He that gadred styckes on the Sabot daye was stoned unto the dethe. And for one grutched ayenst theyr mayster Moyses, the whiche was but *Pedagogus*, the chosen woman moost accepte, Maria, Aaron's sister, was smytten of God with the infyrmyte of leprehode. How ofte tymes breke we our holy daye! How oft tymes grutche we ayenst our maysters, not holdynge us content with noo kynge, nother prynce, archebysshopp, nor bysshopp; beynge as varyaunt as the mone! [The Old Law.] And yet the good Lorde spareth us. The old lawe was harde to observe; in the whiche tyme God entreatyd mankynde after his wrath and punysshement. Wherfore he was callyd *Deus ulcionum*, for whoos delyver mercy cryed to almyghty God to sende mankinde a newe mayster that sholde entreate hym and teche more curtously; and it lyked hym, *Non ex operibus justiciæ quæ fecimus nos, sed secundum suam misericordiam*, (Ad Titum iij°.) to come downe [The New hymself and toke on hym oure mortallyte, gave us a newe lawe, Law.]

ᵃ *i. e,* lending.

wold suffre none but hymselfe to be oure mayster; where with all
love and benygnyte, without sharpnesse, he taught us noo rude
nother grose erthly doctrynes, as they were taughte in the olde
lawe; but he taughte us subtyll thynges, hevenly dyvynytee, oure
glory and oure blysse (*Docebat eos de regno Dei*).   And as longe as
we bene in the scole of mercyfull benygnytee and gentylnesse, though
we doo fawtes, purposynge to amende, soo longe he abydeth us
pacyently, holdynge hymself content.   For by cause we bene now in
mannes state and parfyght age with oure owne correccyon (*Prop-
terea expectat Deus ut misereatur vestri* (Ysaye tricesimo.)   And yf we
dyfferre and wyll not correcte our selfe here in the scole of mercy,
full grevously and moost sharply shall we abyde the swerde of correccyon of his ryghtwysnesse, as dayly by experyence we maye fele.
Therfore, in the thre ages of oure lyfe lette us besye ourselfe to
prayse God wyth pure childerne, amendynge our lyfe by dedes of
penaunce and vertuouse dedes usynge, exhortynge you with the
wordes of my tyme ª—*Laudate, pueri, Dominum.*

The fourme and the maner how that we sholde worshyp and love
almyghty God in the thre Ages, that is to saye, in Childehode,
Yongthe, and Manhode, is shewed to us by a prety conceyte of oure
comyn Kalender in every boke of servyce.   Ye shall understande [The Kalen-
that every moneth noted in the Kalender is dyvyded in thre partyes, dar.]
that is to say *Kalendas, Nonas,* and *Ydus.*   The fyrst daye of every
moneth is called and named *Kalendas;* the seconde is namyd, not
Kalendas, but *quarto, quinto,* or *sexto Nonas,* and soo tyll ye come
to *Nonas;* and after *Nonas,* the dayes bene namyd *Ydus* tyll ye come
to the myddell, and thenne all the moneth after named *Kalendas*
after certen nombres; as the myddes of the monthe is namyd *xix.*
other *xviii. Kalendas,* countynge lesse tyll ye come to the ende.
Morally by these thre, *Kalendas, Nonas,* and *Ydus,* is understande
the thre Ages of Man.   By *Kalendas* is understande Childhode;
Kalendæ is as moche to saye *quasi colendo,* for the consuetude of the

---

ª *i. e.* theme (or text).

Romaynes was, the fyrste daye of the moneth that is called *Kalendas* falleth, to solempnyse to ther goddes Hely, Juno et Jupyter. So verely the childehode of man is dedycate to devocyon. Thenne sette the faders the childerne to scole; and thenne be they taughte to serve God, to saye grace, to helpe the preest to synge; for to be meke, gentyll, and lowely. Thenne saye they our Lady matens, and bene ryght devoute. Of whom may be verefyed that is wryten by Davyd— *Hæc est generacio quærencium Dominum*, that is the generacyon that besyly by devocyon seke almyghty God.

By the seconde daye that is callyd *Nonas* I understande the seconde age, that is callyd *Juventus*, Youthe. *Nonæ dicuntur quasi nullæ*, for in that daye the Romayns worshypt no Goddes, nother in that season was noo festyvall dayes; or elles *nonæ dicuntur quasi nundinæ*, as moche to saye as a fayer, for in that tyme they occupied themself in fayers and marchaundyses. And herto convenyently may be the Youthe of man applyed, that is in specyall from xiiij. yeres unto xviij., in the whiche he is ful of undevocyon, and all moost forgetith to worshyp his God or ony saynt. And yf he do it with his mouthe, his herte is ful ferre from God aboute worldly vanytees. As it is wryten, *Populus hic labiis me honorat, cor autem eorum longe est a me* (*Ysay.* xxix°.) Congruently also Youthe maye be namyd *Nonæ* i. *nundinæ*—a fayer or market, for in this age is the marchaundyse of the devyll. The worlde habundauntly bought. Here the yonge man byeth a strompettes body for his body and soule. Here all vayne marchaundyses of the worlde bene bought, to the whiche is very prone and redy oure youthe of Englonde, as we may see dayly. There is no vanyte in no partye of the worlde but we bene redy to bye it: longe heres and shorte collers of Almayns; evyll fasshenyd garmentes and devyllisshe shoone and slyppers of Frensmen; powches and paynted gyrdylles of Spaynardes; newe founde hattes of Romayns; and so is fulfylled the wordes of oure Lord wryten in holy scrypture (Jeremiæ xi°.), *Elongaverunt a me, et ambulaverunt post vanitatem, et vani facti sunt.* "This Youthe (sayth our Lorde,) hath ferre put hymselfe fro me, and they have

[Childhood dedicate to devotion.]

[Our Lady Matins.]

[The Age of Youth.]

[Fairs and merchandise.]

[The Youth of England.]
[Vanities of Dress.]

walked after theyr owne vanytees, and by theyr invencyons they bene
all vayne and undoubtyd." This alterable vanytees in garmentes is
a true argument and a faythfull conclusyon to all wyse straungers
that Englysshemen bee as chaungable in theyr maners and wyttes [Englishmen changeable.]
as they be in outwarde garmentes. And yf this vayne marchaundyse
were oonly in youth of the reame it were more tollerable, but *invete-
rati dierum malorum,* boyes of fyfty yere of age are as newe fangled
as ony yonge men be. The whiche by reasons holde torne theyr face
from the worlde, consideryng the ende of theyr lyfe. But lytell
that is consydered; ye, rather in theyr vanytees they bene praysed.
*Quoniam laudatur peccator in desideriis animæ suæ, et iniquus bene-
dicitur. (Psalmo, etc.)*

  And the thyrde daye is callyd *Ydus,* the whiche is asmoche to saye [The latter age
as *divisio,* a departynge. By whom I understande the latter age of of Man.]
man, in the whiche man is dyvyded from the worlde by dethe, to
the ende for to receyve good or evyll as he hath deserved in this
present lyfe. Lyke wyse thenne, as in the fyrst part of the moneth
there is but one daye that is callyd *Kalendæ,* the whiche is the
fyrste daye of all, but in the later ende there be many dayes that
bene named of the worde *Kalendas,* so, in comparyson of the fyrst
daye of thy lyfe, that is to say of thy childehode, in the whiche
thou wert well disposyd in devocyon, multeplye thy good lyf and
holy dysposycyon in thy latter dayes, that thou mayest deserve oure
Lordes mercy, sayenge with the Prophete in the sawter, *Et senectus
mea in misericordia uberi.* And how be it thou hast often before in
thy yonge age and myddell age dyvydyd thy lyfe somtyme to
vertue, somtyme to vyce, ye as now in thy latter age kepe thy lyfe
holy in vertue. Dyvyde it no more tyll dethe dyvyde it, after the
counsell of the Gospelles, Joh'is xix°: *Non scindamus eam, sed sor-
ciamur de ea cujus sit*—" Lete us not cutte it, but lete us draw lottes
whose it shall be." How be it this texte after the letter is understonde of Crystys cote without seme, yet convenyently it may be
understonde of every mannys lyfe or soule—*Tunica dicitur quasi tua*

unica.[a]   Whether is more surer thyne owne than thy soule, for the
whiche prayeth the Prophete,[b] sayeng, *Erue a framea, Deus, animam
meam, et de manu canis unicam meam.*   And whyle it is so that man
lyveth here in two lyves, one lyvynge after the pleasur of the worlde,
the tother lyvynge here in vertue by grace to come to blysse, tho
that woll geve one partye of theyr lyfe to vyces and another to vertue,
and specially in theyr age, thyse maner of men dyvyde theyr
cote, and they, nother all the tayllers in the worlde, shall never
make it hole ayen; for, as saynt Jerome sayth in a pystle, *Difficile,*
*ymmo impossibile est, ut quis in præsenti et in futuro fruatur gaudiis,
ut hic ventrem et ibi mentem, et de deliciis transiat*—" It is harde, ye
it is impossyble, that a man may have alle joye in this worlde and
also in heven—here to fylle his body and there to fylle his mynde;"
for truly the delytes of this worlde and the joyes of heven can never
be togyder in one cote of thy soule.   Wherfore yf thy cote of thy
soule be ones hoole in vertue, without ony seme of vice, departe it
never, but lete it retorne *in sortem Domini,* and contynewe thy
lyfe in goodnesse without ony interrupcyon. And lyke wyse as in thy
childehode thou begannest vertue oonly, where thrugh in that age
thou praysest almyghty God, so in thy myddell age, all wanton
vanytees layed apart, encresse thy vertu as tho dyde of whom it 'is
wryten, *Ibunt de virtute in virtutem quousque videatur Deus.*   And
that the ende may be conformable to his pryncyple without dyvy-
sion, followynge the wayes of Innocency with thyse holy Innocents,
in whose commendacions syngeth our moder holy chirche, *Novit
Dominus viam Innocentum qui non steterunt in viis peccatorum.*   And
yf we be in synne to repare ourselfe to the state of grace without
wyll to falle agayn. And in recognysaunce of this gracyous benefyte
of remyssyon we may lovyngly prayse God as I exhortyd you

---

[a]   This was a favourite mode of playing upon the sound of words taken in combination.
Saint Augustine was quoted as authority for *monumentum* being derived, " eo quod
moneat mentem."   See Weever's Discourse of Funerall Monuments, p. 9.
  [b]   Jeremiah.

before, sayeng, *Laudate, Pueri, Dominum*, graunt us all, *Cryste Jhesus Splendor Patris, corona Innocencium.*

AMEN.

Explicit sermo ista.

Note.—The remaining pages of the original pamphlet are filled up with a copy (in Latin) of the Indulgences granted by Pope John XXII., as written up at Rome in the Church of the Blessed Mary called Ara Cœli; but which, as foreign to the present subject, it has not been thought desirable to reprint.

Opposite the last page is a large cut of the Crucifixion.

SERMON OF THE CHILD BISHOP,

PRONOWNSYD BY JOHN STUBS, QUERESTER,

ON CHILDERMAS DAY, AT GLOCETER, 1558.

(Cotton. MS. Vespasian A. xxv., pp. 173—179.)

Nisi conversi fueritis, et efficiamini sicut parvuli, non intrabitis in regnum celorum. MATHEI 18. "Except yow will be convertyd, and made lyke unto lytill childern, yow shall not entre in to the kyngdom of heaven."

AMONG all the conclusions in holy Scripture, which are many and marvellous, Ryght worshypfull audience, this is not the lest to be marvellyd at, doubtyd, and dreadyd of all yow that are no childer, but men, women, and yonggolds, of years and discretion, yow specially whych alow no construction of the Scriptures but only the letter as it lyeth, thys I say whych our Saviour Chryst pronouncyd wyth his own mouth saying, "Except yow wil be convertyd," etc. As he wold say, Lytill ones shall entre to the kyngdom, but other shall not; and so all seme to be excludyd from the kyngdom but only childer, and such as are litill ones lyke unto childer.

Now, to yow that hange of the letter and not of the sprite, this change, for a great one to be changed into a lytill one, and an old man to becum a babe agayne, may seme no lesse strange and impossible to yow, then dyd the mystery of regeneracion, or new birth, unto Nichodemus, when he said unto Christ, *Quomodo potest homo nasci cum sit senex? Numquid potest in ventrem matris suæ iterato introire et renasci?* "How kan a man be born when he is ones old? Is it possible for hym to torne in to his mother's wombe agayne, and

so be borne anew, and becum of an old man a child agayne?" For
other maner of birth then was by nature Nicodemus thaught not of.
But our Saviour Christ gave hym to understand eare he went, that
ther was a birth spirituall in water and in the Holy Goost, which
now is dayly usyd of the Churche in the sacrament of baptisme,
after the which birth it is possible for all ages both yong and old to
be borne agayne anew, and so to have an entre into the kyngdom of
heaven.

In lyke maner understand yow this conclusion of our Saviour, not,
as the letter soundeth, by a miraculos or monstruose conversion of a
man in to a childe as touching age, stature, an discretion, but of a
morall conversion, as touching certyn evill maners that are reprovyd
in men, and other contrary maners which are comendyd in childer,
by which means it is possible ynough for the greatest of men to
becum as litill childer, and for the eldest of women to becum in lyknes
of maners as young babes, which are symple, withowt gyle, innocent,
wythowt harme, and all pure wythowt corruption, as few above the
age of childer are, and as all ought to be, and of necessitie must be
if thei intend ther salvacion according to the wordes of Christ afore
rehersed, *Nisi conversi fueritis*, etc. "Except you wil be convertyd
and be made lyke unto litell ones, you shall not entre into the
kyngdom of heavyn, you shall not entre, you shall not." Marke
and regard the infallible sentence of Christes own mouth. Love
litill ones, therfor, and learn of them how you may have an entre
into the kyngdom of heavyn.

There is another conclusion in Scripture also which semeth to
make as much for men and agaynst childer, to exclude them from
the kyngdom. *Regnum* (inquit) *celorum vim patitur, et violenti
rapiunt illud.* "The kyngdom of heaven (saith our Saviour Christ) ^{Math. 11.}
suffreth violence, and thei that cum by it pluk it unto them with
violence." Now, if this violence stode by strong hand, and force
of bodily strength, alak! what force, what violence, and what
shyfftes could the litill ones make to catch the kingdom unto them?
Every body would pluk it from the litill ones; but, thanks be unto

God! the litill ones have by nature what the elder have by wrestlyng and stryvyng with their own affections. Thei have humilitie of mynd and sprite, which vertue the lower yt goeth the nerer it approcheth the kyngdom of heaven, and other like virtues the childer have which are degrees to the kyngdom; or, if yow understand these wordes of such spirituall violence, which consisteth more in violent suffryng then in violent action or doyng, this conclusion excludeth nether men, women, nor childer, for every one may suffre such kynd of violence for the kyngdom of God.

Such violence usyd thei which, utterly forsakyng the pleasures of the flesh, dyd castrate themselves for the kyngdom of heaven, as our Saviour saith in the 19. chap. of S. Mathew. Such violence usyd the Apostles, which utterly renownsyd the world and all worldly goodes, and folowyd Christ in povertie of the world, and of the sprite both, for the desyre of the kyngdom. Such violence usyd S. Mathew the puplicane, and Mary Magdalene the synner, and all other which, for the love of the kyngdom, do willingly forsake their evill trade and synfull lyving,[a] stryvyng with the world and with themselves to entre into the kyngdom by the narow gate that Christ speke of in the 13. cap. of S. Luke, saying, *Contendite intrare per angustam portam.* "Stryve to entre in by the narow gate."

Such violence usyd our Saviour Christ hym selfe to entre into his own kyngdom, for thus he saith of hymself, *Nonne oportuit Christum pati, et ita intrare in gloriam suam?* "Dyd it not behove Christ to suffre as he dyd, and so to entre into his own kyngdom?" He suffryd this violence not only on the crosse, being at man's state, but also in his cradell, and in his mother's armes in his childhode and infancy, when kyng Herode conspiryd his death, and thought by all meanes to destroy hym in his childhode, but he myst of hym then, as the wyll of God his father was, by flying the persecution in to Ægypt untill the deth of Herode.

---

[a] rs thei dyd, takyng penance upon them, and professyng a new lyfe opynly, not regardyng what the world wold talke or judge of them, but what was expedient for their salvation, as men that dyd stryve, &c. *These words are erased in the MS.*

By such violence these blessyd Innocentes atchyvyd to the kyngdom of heaven, of whom the Church this day make worthy memory. Thei suffryd the violence of Herode and his tormentors, beyng harmless Innocentes deservyng nothing lesse then such cruell death. Yet thei that sawght Christes bloud, beyng uncerteyn of Christys person, dyd onmercifully spill the bloud of all Innocentes that were about the age of Christ, from ij. years old and inward, by means wherof ther death was and is imputed to them for acceptable martyrdom; for the tyrant and his tormentors, beyng oncertyn of Jesus' person, thaught that thei slew the child and innocent Jesus in every of these Innocentes, so that, if thei myst hym in one, thei thought to hitt hym in another. And so every of these Innocentes dyd shed their bloud, not only in the quarell of Christ, but also in the person of Christ, which was a prerogative above all other martyrs; for, allthough many holy martyrs have dyed in the quarell of Christ, yet dyd never none but these blessyd Innocentes dye for the person of Christ; and this is their prerogative in martyrdom, beside the rightuosness of their most pure innocency, withowt the which the suffryng of ther bloud shed and their quarell for Christ cold not gyve them the glory of martyrdom, for a malefactor that suffreth not innocently, but for his own gilt and deservyng, is worthy that he suffreth, saith S. Peter, and he byds such to be content, and to loke for no thankes of God at all. 1ª Petri, 2º.

And so, by this reason of S. Peter, it is evident that thei are far wyde of true martirdom, and consequently of the kyngdom too, which suffryd violence of fyre, hangyng, headyng, banysshyng, or other just execution, for many and divers enormities in ther faith and maners, allthough, in the opinion of ther favorars, thei are taken for very holy martyrs only for ther pretensyd good quarell and for ther patient suffryng, lackyng the commendacion of innocency, which unto martirdom, as I said, is a vertue most necessary: so necessary that withowt it ther is no perfitt charity, withowt the which no cause, no payne, no pacience, no quarell, no, not the quarell of faith and Christ, avayleth or profiteth to the title of mar- [Reflections on the Protestant martyrs.]

tyrdom, or to the title of the kyngdom. This is not my judgement, but S. Augustine's in his boke *De fide, ad Petrum.*

[Abel the first martyr.]   And, for the more prayse of innocency, note you this, that the first Martyr of the world was all an Innocente. Was not Abel, the 2. son of Adam, slayn and martyrryd of his brother Cain at the begynnyng ? He was. Rede the 4. cap. of Genesis. *Et propter quod occidit fratrem suum ?* " And why dyd the wicked Cain slay his brother ?" saith S. John. *Quia opera ejus maligna erant, fratris autem ejus justa.* " Because (saith he) that his own workes were evill, and his brother's workes were good." And so it appereth that Abell suffered in the quarell of his innocency, and so he is termyd Abell the innocent, and the first Martyr.

['The Innocents the first martyrs after the birth of Christ.]   Note you agayne that the first martyrs in the new law after the birth of Christ were a nombre of Innocentes togythers which all suffryd for ther innocency, because thei were found in that state of innocency that Jesus was hymselfe; wheras, if thei had been out of that state, and those years of innocency which agreed with the age of Jesus, they had not suffryd; but it was not without the great providence of God that these first martyrs should be all innocentes.

[Stephen the first martyr after the death of Christ.]   Thridly. Note yow that the first martyr that ever was after the death of Christ was S. Steven; but the same was an innocent too, for, while his enymyes that saught his death could fynd no cause in hym worthy of death, the text saith that they dyd subornate false wittnesses that chargyd hym with blasphemy, and for blasphemye he dyed, wherin he was most innocent. Vide the 6. of the Actes, there shall you find it.

[All true martyrs innocents.]   Brefely, all the martirs that ever were alowyd and approvyd for trew and holy Martyrs in dede were all Innocentes, giltles of ther death, by no meanes deservyng the same on ther own behalfe.

Thus much I have said of the virtue of innocency, for the honor of these blessyd Innocentes and innocent childer, which are remem-
[Childermas day.]   bryd in the Church this day; which day, as it is commynly termed Childermas day, so is it celebrate and solempnisyd by the preferment of childer in all great cathedrall churches, which gyve the

childer the prerogative this day above men, in token that the innocent childer which shed ther bloud for the person of the most pure
innocent child Jesus had a prerogative above all men in ther kind
of martyrdom, as I said before. Of this vertue of innocency, and
other vertues and good properties in childer, which are to be folowyd
of the elders, I purpose to speke more largely in my processe; and,
that I may have the grace this to expresse for your edificacion, and
yow the grace the same to beare away and folow for your own weale
and salvacion, so that, on my part and yours both, all may redownd
to the honor and glory of Allmighty God, before I wade any farder
in this matter I shall desyre you all to assist me with your prayer.

Preces.

A-A-A- *domine Deus, ecce nescio loqui quia puer ego sum.* O [Prayer.]
Lord, which namest thyself Alpha et O, the first letter and the
last, the begynnyng and the end of all thinges, and consequently of
all wordes that may be writtyn or spoken by any letters, from the
first letter to the last, behold I have begon to speke unto thy people
as it were at the first lettre—helpe me that I may go through to the
end, for, consideryng my tendre age and infansy, I am constrayned
to complayn with the wordes of the prophete Jeremy, *s.* A-A-A- Cap. 1ᶜ.
Lord God, behold I kan not speke, I kan not utter thy wordes and
thy message as besemeth, *quia puer ego sum,* because I am but a child,
not only as Jeremye was, but I am a child in dede; but, if I were
a man that had utterance and eloquence to set forth and prosecute
thi word, which I have begon with all in my theme towchyng the
change of men into childer, Lord, how earnest I wold be with the
elders of this audience to convert them selves and ther maners to
the lykness of litill childer, that thei myght be suer of thy gloriose
kyngdom. Lord, how fervent I wold be with my late companions,
yong boys, which yet beare the name of childer, to retagne and
kepe the commendable qualities of childer, and not to degenerate
from ther vertues, that I myght make them also partenars of thy
kyngdom. But I am a very child in these matters, and kan not
speake halfe perfectly. Thow knoest, O Lord!

[Exhortation.]   What then, good people? Because I kan not speake perfectly and eloquently shall I speake nothing at all? Why am I set up-in this place? Why is the message committed unto me? Speake I must, allthough lyke a child, and stammer owt of this word of God a briefe exhortacion to both sortes, the elders and yongers, as well as I kan; first to the elders, and after to the yongers; and, that don, as brefely as I kan comprise, I shall committ yow to God.

[First to the elders.]   First, therfor, of these wordes of our Saviour, " Except yow wil be convertyd and becum as litill childer, yow shall not entre into the kyngdom of heavyn," I gather this lesson for yow that are of the elder sort, that of necessitie yow must nede reforme your corrupt maners, which are dissonant and disagreable with the incorrupt maners of childer, and frame your affections thereafter, so that yow be convertyd into the better, or else you kan not loke for the kyngdom of heaven; for th'Apostles them selves, in the tyme of ther carnalitie and imperfection, contending among them selfes for the highest roume in the kyngdom, and which of them should be more worthy then other, were answeryd with the same wordes that yow all are, that, except thei would becum other maner a men, and be convertyd into the lykeness of childer by humilitie and other vertues, thei should have no part in the kyngdom of Christ.

The apostles upon this framyd them selves accordingly for the love of the kyngdom, and thei understode by the answer that the kyngdom of heavyn wold not be gotten by pride, ambition, contencion, envy, emulacion, stowtness, and elacion; therfor they abasyd them selves to most profound humilitie, povertie, mekeness of sprite; and convertyd ther maners most like to the maners of innocent childer. Therfor considre what behoveth yow for your partes that, seth the apostles, were forsyd thus to do by the answer of Christ, what behoveth yow to do on your behalfe for the love of the kyngdom. Yow must nede gyve over your stowt corage that bolden yow to syn, and yow must becum meke as childer; if yow will cum to heavyn yow must not disdayn to becum and to be cowntyd as childer.

But how as childer? Not to be childysh in witt, understandyng, and discrecion; for S. Pawl, the secretary of Christ's cownsell, do cownsell the contrary in the 4. cap. to the Ephesians, *Ne simus sicut parvuli fluctuantes qui circumferantur omni vento doctrinæ*, etc. " Let us not be still as childer that be wavering and wilbe caried hyder and thyder with every blast of doctrine," by the wylynes and craftynes of men which lay wayt to deceive us. Yf we note these wordes of S. Pawl well, you shall perceive that he takes it to be a childysh poynt for any Christian man to waver in his faith, and that it is for lak of witt if he be caried from the doctrine of his awncient relligion in to a new fanglyd doctrine, which hath no suertie in it, but is inconstant as the wynd. Yf this be a childysh poynt, and argueth lak of witt [Waverers in and discrecion, as S. Pawl saith, I report me to you how many their faith of late years.] witless childer and childysh people were in thys realme of late years and yet are in many places, which waveryd in ther faith, and were caried hyder and thyder, from one opinion to another, as childer ar caried with an apple, or wyth a puffe of wynd, as thei that have strength to resist nothing, which is reproveable in men that should have constancie and discrecion.

Therfor S. Pawl in an other place saith thus, *Nolite effici pueri* 1 Cor. 14. *sensibus*, " Be yow not childer as touching witt and discrecion," *sine malitiis parvuli estote*, " but as touching malice and syn be yow not only as childer, but as litill litill childer," that kan not tell what syn or malice meanith.

Considre well the nature of innocent childer, and yow shall perceive in them no maner of malice, no envy, no disdayne, no hurtfullness, no synfull affection, no pride, no ambition, no singularitie, no desyre of honor, of riches, of carnalitie, of revenginge, or quittyng evyll for evyll; but all the affections quiet, in all pacience, in all simplicitie, in all puritie, in all tractableness, in all obedience, in all humilitie, and in all innocency; and no such synfull affections reigning in them as commynly rageth in men and women of years.

These and such other good qualities in childer are to be observyd and folowed of yow that are the elders; but specially, and among all other vertues, I wold wish yow to embrace the innocency of childer, for that one vertue includeth all, as the generall includeth the spe-

ciall, for who that hath this innocency hath halfe the rightuosness
and perfection of a Christian man's lyfe; for the rightuosness of lyfe
growndyd in the rightuosness of fayth resteth upon ij. poyntes which
the prophet Esai expresseth by thes wordes, *Quiescite agere perversè,
discite bene facere,* " Cease to do evill and learn to do well." Who
that observes the first part is an innocent, if he cease to do evill;
who that observes the 2. part is a just man, if he learne and practise
to do well.

The same is expressed by the prophete David in these wordes,
Declina a malo, et fac bonum, " Shon the evill, and do the good."
The shonning of evill belonges to the innocent; the doing of good
belonges to the just man. The first is expressyd agayne by the vertuose man Tobie, saying to his son, *Quod oderis tibi fieri hoc alteri
unquam ne feceris,* " What thing thow wold not have done to thy
selfe that thyng never do unto other." Mark this part for the innocent. The other part is expressyd by our Saviour hymselfe, Luc. 6.
saying, *Prout vultis ut faciant vobis homines et vos facite illis similiter,*
" Evyn as yow desire that other should do to yow, do yow the same
good unto them." Lykewise marke this part for the rightuose man.

Now compare yow the ij. partes togyder, and se how far or how
nere yow are to the kyngdom of heavyn. If yow have both these
partes of rightuosness yow are very nere to the kyngdom, and the
kyngdom is nere unto yow. Yf yow have but the first part only,
which standeth by innocency, then are yow halfe the way to the
kyngdom. Yf yow have nother the one part nor the other, and hold
yow ther, then are yow from the kyngdom so farr as thei that shall
never cum ther: therfor loke well unto it ; and remembre the wordes
of our Saviour, that except yow wilbe convertyd and chaungyd, and
becum lyke unto litill childer, yow shall not entre into the kyngdom
of heavyn. And this I have said as touching the first part for yow
that be the elders.

[Address to the children.] Now for yow childer, both boys and wenches, that beare the name
of childer, I gather this lesson of the wordes of our Saviour, that it
is for yow most necessary to kepe the innocency of your childhod,
and other vertues proper unto that tendre age, and not to learn the

vices and evill qualities of your elders, leste yow lose the kyngdom which is appoynted unto yow by name. And tyme it is to call upon yow this to do, for not only I, but the world, do se in yow that yow and the very litill ones that follow yow do grow nowadayes so fast owt of this innocent state that it is wonder to me to se amonge yow so many childer in years, and so few innocentes in maners. I am not very old my selfe to speake by experience; but I have hard say of my elders that a child was wont to continew an innocent untill he [How long a child continues an innocent.] was 7. years old, and untill 14. years he was provyd to be of such vertue and honest nurture that he deservyd the love and prayse of all people; and now we shall not fynd such a one at 7. as was then at 14, nor at 5. as was then at 7, nor scant at 3. as was then at 9. or x. years old : this is great odes, but is this a good hearyng? Tell me, yow boys, yow childer, yow litill ones, are yow not ashamyd of your partes that yow are so sone corruptyd? so sone ripe, and so sone rottyn? so late innocentes, and so sone lewd lads? deservyng nother love nor prayse of any honest person. What yow are I kan not tell; but, a my honestie, I am both ashamyd of it and sory for it, that yow should so slandre the name of childer, and deceive your elders, which have an eye unto yow to note and folow your maners, as thei are advertysed by the wordes of Christ.

Good people, yow know your charge by the wordes of Christ how that yow must of necessitie be convertyd if yow will enjoy the kyngdom of heavyn, and how yow are sent to these childer to take example of your conversion to the better; and I have partly exhortyd yow here unto; and now the childer that should be for your example [Children now evil mannered and corrupted.] are so evill maneryd for the most part, and so vitiosly corruptyd in ther maners, that I will not wish yow to folow them, except it be upon great choyse and great discrecion; and yet some I must appoynt unto yow for example.

But wher shall I fynd them? In the citie? I dare not warrant [The children of the City.] yow to folowe the childer of the citie, no not the yongest of all, if thei be ones owt of ther mothers' handes and kan run abowt the streates and speake all thinges perfittly; for thei have be scolyd at home that of them as yong as thei are yow may learne as evill properties

as yow have all redy of your own; yea and perhapps the same which
the child learnyd of yow before, as to swere with a grace, as som
termes the othes that cum from the hart, with a stomake to curse
bitterly, to blaspheme, to lye, to moke ther elders, to nyckname ther
æqualls, to knowledge no dutie to ther betters, and such other
many mo. Thei go to scole in the open streates one with an other.
I will not wysh yow to folow such.

[Children of the Grammar Schools.]
Which then? The childer that go to scole in the grammer scoles
under a master? A man wold think yea, because thei are scoles set
up purposly for the good educacion of childer, as well in good nurture as in good learning; but yet I dare not warant yow to folow the
childer of the grammer scoles, for, how so ever it happ, nurturyd thei
are as evill or rather worse then the other. Yf yow will have a
profe herof, mark ther maners in the temple, and at the table;
mark ther talkes and behavior by the wayes at such tymes and houres
as thei leave scole and go home to ther meales, specially on holydays
and campos dayes,[a] when thei are sett a litill at libertie. I will say no
more; but mark them, for I have lost my mark except yow find the
most of them most ongracious grafftes, ripe and redy in all lewd
libertie. I will not wish yow to folow such.

[The choristers and children of the Song School.]
Which then? The queresters and childer of the song-scole? Beware
what yow do: for I have experience of them more then of the other.
Yt is not so long sens I was one of them myself but I kan remembre
what shrewness was used among them, which I will not speake of
now;[b] but I kan not let this passe ontouched how boyyshly thei be-
have themselves in the church, how rashly thei cum into the quere
without any reverence; never knele nor cowntenaunce to say any
prayer or Pater noster, but rudely squat down on ther tayles,[c] and
justle wyth ther felows for a place; a non thei startes me owt of
the quere agayne, and in agayne and out agayne, and thus one

[a] Campus, or camp-days, for matches at football.

[b] *As first written*, what fightyng, lying, mooching, and forgyng of false excuses was
among them, beside that, where thei are brought up specially to serve God in the church,
thei do nothing lesse in the church then serve God.

[c] which lak twynggyng, *erased.*

after an other, I kan not tell how oft nor wherfor, but only to gadd and gas abrode, and so cum in agayne and crosse the quere fro one side to another and never rest, withowt any order, and never servo God nor our Lady with mattyns or with evynsong, no more then thei of the grammer scoles; whose behaviour is in the temple as it were in ther scole ther master beyng absent, and not in the church God being present. I will not wysh you to folow such.

Which then?   Here is a company afore me of childer, semely in sight, most like unto innocentes, specially one litill one in the mydes, [One little one in the midst.] which puts me in mynd of the child which Jesus callyd unto hym and set in the myd of his disciples when they were at bate who should be chefe among them; the child had prayse of Jesus' own mouth for his meke behaviour and nurture, so much that Jesus said of him, *Quique se humiliavit sicut parvulus, iste intrabit in regnum celorum,* "Who so that meke and humble hym selfe as this child doth here before yow, he shall entre into the kyngdom of heaven."   Such a one this litill one in the mydes here appereth to be that he myght be thought worthy to be sett in the mydes for an example unto yow of pure childhode, mekness, and innocency. Loke in his face and yow wold think that butter wold not melt in his mouth; but, as smothe as he lokes, I will not wysh yow to folow hym if yow know as much as I do.   Well, well! all is not gold that shynes, nor all are not innocentes that beare the face of childer.

Now I se non other choyse but that I must leave the boys and the childer that are ripe in witt and speche, and must poynt yow to the litill ones which yet run on ther mother's hand, onable of them selfes to run strongly abrode, as yet onrype in witt and onperfitt in speche: sett your eye upon such and observe in them the true vertues of a child for your example, for such I dare warant yow. As for the residue, I dare not warant yow, except it be one among a C., whom yow must chewse with great observacion and discrecion.

Here is a great lake and small choyse among so many childer: and where is the falte? wher is the great falte? Evyn in yow that are ther parents, ther fathers, mothers, and ther scolemasters. [The great fault is want of teaching.]

ᵃ Where is the great falte? Evyn in the parentes, fathers, mothers
and scolemasters, which do nother teach ther childer good, nother
yet chastice them when thei do evill; when thei lye and swere as I
have hard some do, Good Lord, how abominably! and curse with
plages and pestilence and murrens upon ther felows, brothers, and
sisters, evyn ther parentes standyng by and hearing them; and yet
not a word of correction, notwithstandyng thei have a great care and
charge upon ther childer as thei know ther folies, and shall gyve a
straight accompte for them unto allmyghtie God.   And what is the

[Fond and foolish affection of parents] matter? a folysh affection and a fond opinion in the parentes, which
very fondly seke the love of ther child that knoweth not what love
or dutye meaneth, and that he may say " I am father's boy " or " I
am mother's boy," and " I love father (or mother) best; " to wyn this
word, and the love of the child, the parentes contend who shall make
most of the child, and by these means no partye dare displease hym,
say he or do he never so ongraciously, but both parties dandill hym
and didill hym and pamper hym and stroke his hedd and sett hym
a hye bence, and gyve hym the swetyst soppe in the dish evyn when
he lest deserve it: this marrs the child, it makes hym to thynke he
does well when he do stark nought.

There are very fond fathers in this poynt, and many mo fond mothers.   Dyd you never here, yow fond mothers, what the wise Salomon saith, *Qui parcitur virgæ odit filium,* " Thei that spare the rodd
do hate the child:" and yet yow that never use the rod wyll say that
yow do it for love toward your child.   The wyse man sayth such love
is hatered; therfor it must nede be a fond love that you beare toward your childer in this poynt, specially in such mothers as when
ther childer do a falt, and never so many faltes, which will not ones
touch the child, but take the rod and beate the quyssion or the forme

[Fond mothers beat the cushion or form, and burn the rod.] and after borne the rodd and say thei spare not the rodd.   O fond,
fond mothers! what falt have the quyssion don to be bettyn? what
falt have the rodd don to be brent?   Your child have done the falt,

---

ᵃ This commences another sheet of the MS.

why do not he smart of the rodd? Why do you spare the child? What hurt kan the rodd do to your child? Ys it not an old and a tru saying, *The rodd breakes no bones?* But you have such a fond tendrenes that yow kan not fynd in your hart to beat your tendre-lyng, for if he should wepe yow must wepe to for company. Well, I wyll take upon me now to be a prophete in this matter, that such mothers shall wepe here after to see the ontowardness of such childer, when the childer will not wepe with the mothers for company as yow mothers do now with them.

The fathers are as fond agayne on the other part: " Nay, (say [The fathers thei,) yf I should beate my child, and kepe hym undre and in awe will not kill the courage of their now, I should kill his corage in his youth, and take away his hart children.] that he shall never be bold when he is a man." Mary! that is the very thyng that is meanyd in all good educacion, to discorage youth utterly as touching vice and vicious maners, and to bolden and corage them in all probitye and vertue, and vertuose maners. To lake a stomake and boldness in vice is no lake nor disprayse, but prayse and profitt withall; but, yf your desire be to have them stowt in evill demaner, yow shal be the first that shall have experience of that stowtness; for, after a litill time, thei wil be so styfe and stubborn against yow that yow shall not be able to rule them yf yow wold, and, in conclusion, they will contempne yow, and sett yow at nought above all other persons. This is the retorne of such fond tendreness; as experience teacheth by the example of thowsands which have ben brought up so choysely, tendrely, and dangerosly. Well, to be breffe, if yow will know the resolucion of this opinion for stowtness, and for [the end] of such corrupt educacion, rede yow the boke of the son of Syrac, cap. 30. Ther you shall find the matter playn ynowgh agaynst yow, and I wold now recyte it unto yow if it were not to long for this short tyme.

Now, farewell yow fathers and mothers: yow have your lesson. I must have a word or ij. with the scolemaisters, which, at some of your handes, take your childer in cure to teach and nurture them, as well in vertue as in prophane learnyng.

Therfor I say now to yow scolemasters, that have the youth under
your handes to make or marr, marr them not by your neglygence,
but make them to God ward with your diligence.   Remembre that
Allmyghtie God regardeth the litill ones, and wold not have them
to be led from hym by yow, but by yow to be brought unto hym;
and this he will require at your handes, as well as at the parentes,
for your scole is your cure, and yow shall give accomptes for every
scoler in your scole for the tyme beyng; and yow owght to regard
them all as your childer, and your selfes as their fathers, for Quinti-
lian, the flower of scolemasters, termeth you to be *tertios parentes,*
the thred parentes to the child which yow have under your cure for
good educacion; for, as the carnall parentes by carnalitye do fascion
the body, so the scolemaster do or owght to fascion the soule of
the child by good educacion in learnyng of good nurture and vertue;
and therefore the scolemaster that so doth is cowntyd to be the 3.
parent to the child, yea, and the most worthiest parent of the 3, in
as much as the good fascionyng of the soule by nurture and vertue
is better then the best fascionyng of the body by nature; and so the
scolar will regard his scolemaster for ever if he have at his handes
such educacion that he fele hym selfe the better, otherwise he will
contempne hym of all men, evyn as the child brought up in stoutness
will most contempne the father and mother.   Yow scolemasters
have a good order in your scoles for breaking Priscian's head or
syngyng out of tune.   I wold yow wold take the same order for
breakyng of God's comandementes and ontunynge of Godes harpe,
which soundeth in all his wordes.   Yf a scoler of the song scole
syng out of tune, he is well wrong by the ears, or else well beatyn.
Yf a scoler in the gramer scole speak false Lattyn or Englysh for-
byddyn, he is takyn withall of one or the other and warnyd custos
to be beatyn.   I wysh that yow wold take the like order for the
evill behaviour of your scolers, that, if any be takyn with a word of
blasphemy, with a word of ribaudry, with a manifest lye, and such
talke or dedes as are contrary to the laws of God and the holye
Churche, let them be first warnyd custos, or wrong by the ears for

it, and after be correctyd as the custos is usyd.   Other good orders devise of your selves for the good purpose, as yow wyll avoyd the reproche of synfull negligence both before God and man.

Perhaps some will think hert in ther myndes that I am very bold to fynd so many faltes with so many parties—fathers, mothers, scolemasters, childer, scolers, and no scollers; and take upon me to reforme my elders, I beyng so yong in age as I am, and to reprove other wherin I am not all clere my selfe, as some will judge that knew me in my childhode.   Well! if we all amend we shalbe never the worse; and I confesse to them that I was sumtyme, as yet the most of them are, shrewd ynough for one; but I paid well for it, and have now left it, and I may now alledge for my self the wordes of S. Pawl, *Cum essem parvulus, sapiebam ut parvulus, cogitabam ut parvulns, loquebar ut parvulus: nunc autem factus sum vir evacuavi ea quæ erant parvuli:* " When I was a chyldysh boy, my discrecion was therafter, my wordes and dedes were therafter, the fansys and desires of my hart were therafter; but, now that I have cum to be a man, I have cast of all boy's touches," that is to say, all shrowdness of childhod, as I wold all yow had don, retayning the puritie of your childhod, that it may [endure] with yow togyther with age and years, and no doubt that will cause you to grow unto honestie and wor-shippe (as you see in me this day), and also bring yow to the honor and felicitie of the kingdom, which is promised to pure and innocent childer; and, so being, I wold wysh yow to have many folowars, yea, all this holl audience present, that, as thei folow yow in your puritie and innocency, so thei may entre with yow into the kyngdom of everlastyng glorye throwghe the intercession of the holy and blessyd Innocentes, who are the occasion of this my simple collacion this day, and through the merittes of our Saviour Jesus Christ, unto whom, with the Father and the Holy Gost, be all prayse, honor, and glory, for ever and ever!   Amen.

Deo Gratias.

Ex. RIC. RAMSEY.

APPENDIX.

Compotus Nicholay de Newerk custodis bonoꝝ Joħis de Cave Epĩ Innocenciũ Anno dñi ꝉc. Nonagesimo sexto.

In pᵢmis rᵖ de xij đ rᵖ in oblaco͂e die Natĩtatꝑ dñi   Et de
xxiiij s j đ reč in oblač die Innocenĩ ꞇ j coclearͬ argenͭ ponđ xx đ ꞇ j annulũ argenͭ cũ bursa cerica eođ die ad missam   Et de xx đ reč de Maḡro Wiħmo de Kexby p̄centorͬ   Et de ij s reč de Maḡro Joħe de Schirburñ cancellarͬ   Et de vj s viij đ rᵖ de Maḡro Joħ de Newton thesaurarͬ ad Novam ᵃ   Et de vj s viij đ rᵖ de Maḡro Thoma Dalby archiđ Richmũđ   Et de vj s viij đ rᵛ de Maḡro Nichõ de Feriby   Et de vj s viij đ rᵖ de Maḡro Thoma de Wallworth.

Smᵘ lv s v đ.

Iĩm rᵖ de vj s viij đ rᵖ de Dño Abbīe Moñ bĩe Marie v̄ḡ exᵘ
Muros Eboꝝ   Et de iij s iiij đ reč de Maḡro Willħo de Feriby Archiđ Estriđ.

Smᵘ x s.

Iĩm de iij s iiij đ rᵖ de dño Thoma Ugtreht milite   Et de ij s rᵖ
de pⁱore de Kyrkhᵘᵐ   Et de vj s viij đ rᵖ de pⁱore de Malton   Et de xx s rᵖ de comitissa de Northumbͬ ꞇ j anulũ aurͬ   Et de vj s viij đ de pⁱore de Bridlyngtoñ   Et de iij s iiij đ de pⁱore de Watton   Et de iij s iiij đ de rectore de Bayntoñ   Et de iij s iiij đ de Abbīe de Melsa   Et de xx đ rᵖ de pⁱore de Feriby   Et de vj s viij đ rᵖ de dño Stepħo de Scrope   Et de ij s de pⁱore de Drax   Et de vj s viij đ rᵖ de Abbīe de Selby   Et de iij s iiij đ rᵖ de pⁱore de Pontefrač   Et de vj s viij đ rᵖ de pⁱore Sči Oswalđ   Et de

---

ᵃ The meaning of " ad Novam " is doubtful.

iij Ꝥ iiij đ r⁹ de pᶦore de Munkbretton   Et de vj Ꝥ viij đ r⁹ de dño
Joħe Depdene   Et de vj Ꝥ viij đ r⁹ de dña de Marmeon ꝶ j anulū
auꝛ cū bursa cerica   Et de iii Ꝥ iiij đ de dña de Harlsay   Et de
vj Ꝥ viij đ de dña de Rosse   Et de ij Ꝥ r⁹ de Abħte Ryavaħ   Et de
ij Ꝥ r⁹ de Abħte Bellalanđ   Et de ij Ꝥ r⁹ de pᶦore de Novoburgo
Et de xx đ r⁹ de pᶦore de Marton.   Smᶜ v ħi. x Ꞅ.

                        Smᶜ totaɫ Receptoꝝ viij ħi xv Ꞅ v đ.

De quibꝝ dc̄us N. compotat adᵃ "O virgo virginū"   In pane p
speciebꝝ j đ   In Ꝯvisia vj đ.   Smᶜ vij đ.

Iꞇm in sua Cena   In pane vij đ   Et inᵇ pane dñico iiij đ   In
Ꝯviꞅ xxj đ   In carñ vituɫ ꝶ mutuɫ ixđ oƀ   In sawcetiis iiij đ   In
ij anatibus iiij đ   In xij galliñ ij Ꞅ vj đ   In viij wodkoks ꝶ j pluver
ij Ꞅ ij đ   In iij doꞅ ꝶ x feldfars xix đ   In ꝑvis avibus iij đ   In vino
ij Ꞅ iij đ   In divꞅ spēbꝝ xj đ   In lx wardons v đ oƀ   In melle ij đ
oƀ   In cenapio j đ   In ij ħi candeɫ ij đ oƀ   In flouꝛ ij đ   In focali
j đ oƀ   Iꞇm coco vj đ.   Smᶜ xv Ꞅ vj đ oƀ.

Itm̃ die Innocenꞇ ad cenam   In pane iij đ   In Ꝯviꞅ v đ   In
carñ vituɫ ꝶ mutuɫ vij đ   In pipe ꝶ croco j đ.   Diebꝝ vēn⁹is ꝶ sabbī
nichil qᶦa nō visitarūt.   Itm̃ docᶜ pᶦma seq̄nꞇ diebꝝ lune Martę
Mercuꞛ n¹ qᶦa nō visitarūt.   Die Jovis s. die Ocꞇ Innocenꞇ inierūt
versus Kexby ad doᵐ de Ugtrehte ꝶ revenerūt ad cenā   In pane
ij đ   In Ꝯviꞅ iiij đ   In carñ v đ   Diebꝝ vēn⁹is et sabbīi nichil qᶦa
nō visitarūt.   Docᶜ ij⁴ s. die Scī Willm̄i devillaverūt   In pane ad
Jantacɫm ij đ   In Ꝯviꞅ iij đ   In carñ v đ.   Die lune cū ebdoᶜ seq̄nꞇ
nichil qᶦa exᶜ villam.   Docᶜ iij⁴ cū ebdoᶜ seq̄nꞇ exᶜ villam.   Die
sabbī revenerūt ad cenam   In pane j đ oƀ   In Ꝯviꞅ iij đ   In lacte
ꝶ pisc̄ iij đ.   Docᶜ iiij⁴ n¹.   Die lune ineꞛt ad scolas et p̄ Jantacɫ
devillaverūt   In pane ij đ .In Ꝯviꞅ iij đ oƀ   In carñ vij đ.   Die

---

ᵃ One of the nine anthems called "the great O's," and this one was sung at vespers, on
the 23rd of December.

ᵇ This was probably for "the holy loaf."—See Dr. Rock's "Church of Our Fathers,"
i. p. 135.

sabbī revenerūt nd cenā In pane ij đ oƀ In ꝯviꝻ ij đ In piꝺ̃
vj đ. Docᵘ̷ vᵘ̷ usꝗ ad fiñ Purific̃ nˡ. Smᵘ̷ v Ꝼ vij đ oƀ.

In pˡmis In ꝫona empt ꝓ eꝓo iij đ In emendac̃ pilii sui j đ
In pane equino ante arreptꝼ itineris ij đ In oblac̃ aꝑd Bridlyngtoꝛ
ij đ In elemosīa ibiđ j đ In ferilay aꝑd Melsam iiij đ In ferilay
apud Drax iiij đ In pane equino aꝑd Selby iiij đ Itm̃ barbiton-
sori j đ In j. garth aꝑd Bridlyngtoñ j đ In emendac̃ j. garth
ibiđ oƀ In ij pectinibꝫ eqˡnis empꝼ aꝑd Bridlyngtoñ ꞇ Eboꝛ iiij đ
In j. garth aꝑd Beꝟt j đ In ferracõe equoꝫ aꝑd Feriby viij đ oƀ
In emendac̃ j. garth oƀ In cena aꝑd Ledes xvij đ In feno ꞇ
avena ibiđ xiij đ Iꝼ in cena aꝑd Riplay xvj đ In feno et avena
ibiđ xij đ oƀ In ferrac̃ equoꝫ aꝑd Fontans iiij đ In ferilay versꝰ
Harlsay iiij đ In baytyng aꝑd Allertoñ vj đ In vino ꝓ eꝓo viij đ
In pane et feno equoꝫ aꝑd Helmslay vj đ In ferracõe equoꝫ aꝑd
Novūburgū iij đ Smᵘ̷ x Ꝼ vij đ.

In pˡmis In j. torchio ēpꝼ pond xij ƭi. iiij Ꝼ iij đ In j. pilio ix đ
In j. paꝛ cirothecaꝫ lineaꝫ iij đ In j. paꝛ manicaꝫ iij đ In j. paꝛ
cultelloꝫ xiiij đ In j. paꝛ calcaꝛ v đ Iꝼ ꝓ factura robe xviij đ In
furura agnina ēpꝼ ꝓ suptunica ij Ꝼ vj đ In fururis ex convencõne
vj Ꝼ In ꝟicidiis ꝓ totū tēpꝰ viij đ In carboñ mariñ vij đ In
carboñ ligñ x đ In pariꝻ candeꝼ iiij đ oƀ In xxviij paꝛ cirothecaꝫ
ēpꝼ ꝓ vicaꝛ ꞇ maꝑris scolaꝫ iij Ꝼ iiij đ oƀ Iꝼ ꝓ emendac̃ cape cerice
ij đ Smᵘ̷ xxiij Ꝼ j đ.

In pˡmis Nicħo de Newsome tenori suoᵃ xiij Ꝼ iiij đ Et eiđ ꝓ
suo equo conducto ij Ꝼ Iꝼ Roƀto Dawtry senescallo vj Ꝼ viij đ ꞇ ꝓ
ꝑdicõibꝫ ejusđ in capella ij Ꝼ j đ oƀ Iꝼ Joħi Baynton ᵇ cantaꝼ mediū
x Ꝼ Iꝼ Joħi Grene v Ꝼ Iꝼ Joħi Ellay iij Ꝼ iiij đ Iꝼ Joħi Schaptoñ
ꝫvienꝼ eiđ cū ij equis suis x Ꝼ ij đ Iꝼ Thome Marschale ꝓ j. equo
iij Ꝼ iiij đ Iꝼ j. sellaꝛ ꝓ j. equo iij Ꝼ vj đ Iꝼ pistori ꝓ j. equo
iij Ꝼ vj đ Iꝼ Ric̃do Fowleꝛ ꝓ ij equis v Ꝼ. Smᵘ̷ lxvij Ꝼ xj đ oƀ.

ᵃ His tenor voice singer, or, in other words, the leader of his choir.

ᵇ This John Baynton sang the introit of the mass on the Sunday next after Christmas
Day, and this introit begins " Dum medium silentium tenerent omnia," &c.

Feoda m̄st°r' ł ecc'ia m̄st°nc'.

In p̔mis succentoř vicař ij ꝫ sбcancellař xij đ Iꞇ cere p̃uoꝛ ᵃ xij đ Iꞇ c̔ic℘ de vestiб xij đ Iꞇ sacristis xij đ Iꞇ ꝑ ornac̃õe cathedre ep̃aꞇ iiij đ Iꞇ in ligno pro stallis iiij đ Iꞇ in denař c̃õibꝫ xviij đ Itm̃ custodi choristaꝛ iij ꝫ iiij đ.   Sm̄ᵘ xj ꝫ vj đ.

     Sm̄ᵘ toᶫ Expensaꝛ vjꞇi xiiij ꝫ x đ oб Et sic Recepta excedūt expensas xl ꝫ vj đ oб ad usū Ep̃i.

   ᵃ These were small wax tapers carried in procession by the boys in the Boy Bishop's train, or by his so-called "clerks."

www.ingramcontent.com/pod-product-compliance
Lightning Source LLC
Chambersburg PA
CBHW022149090426
42742CB00010B/1433